Praise for

A WALK WITH CHRIST TO THE CROSS

"A WALK WITH CHRIST TO THE CROSS is a must-read for every believer or person with questions about Christianity. In the sprit of his presentation on the radio, Dawson engages the reader and communicates in a way that anyone can understand the message."

—*Todd Shannon, Clear Channel Radio*

"For decades Dawson McAllister has been leading people to the cross, showing them the significance of Christ's sacrifice and the power in His resurrection. A WALK WITH CHRIST TO THE CROSS is that life-changing message and should be shared with everyone you know, whether they have a relationship with Christ or not."

—*Josh D. McDowell, author and speaker*

A WALK WITH CHRIST TO THE CROSS

The Last Fourteen Hours of His Earthly Mission

DAWSON McALLISTER

NEW YORK BOSTON NASHVILLE

Copyright © 2009 Dawson McAllister

All rights reserved. Except as permitted under the U.S. Copyright Act of 1976, no part of this publication may be reproduced, distributed, or transmitted in any form or by any means, or stored in a database or retrieval system, without the prior written permission of the publisher.

Scripture quotations noted TGL are from *Jesus Christ — The Greatest Life: A Unique Blending of the Four Gospels,* Johnston M. Cheney and Stanley Ellisen, ThD, comp. and trans. (Eugene, OR: Paradise Publishing, 1999). Used by permission.

Scripture quotations noted ESV are from The Holy Bible, English Standard Version, copyright © 2001 by Crossway Bibles, a publishing ministry of Good News Publishers. Used by permission. All rights reserved.

Scripture quotations noted KJV are from the King James Version of the Bible.

Scripture quotations noted NIV are from the Holy Bible, New International Version®. Copyright © 1973, 1978, 1984 by International Bible Society. Used by permission of Zondervan Publishing House. All rights reserved.

Scripture quotations noted NASB are from the New American Standard Bible®. Copyright © 1960, 1962, 1963, 1968, 1971, 1972, 1973, 1975, 1977, 1995 by The Lockman Foundation. Used by permission.

Scripture quotations noted NKJV are from the New King James Version ®, copyright © 1979, 1980, 1982 by Thomas Nelson, Inc., Publishers.

Scripture quotations noted NLT are from the *Holy Bible,* New Living Translation, copyright © 1996, 2004. Used by permission of Tyndale House Publishers, Inc., Wheaton, Illinois 60189. All rights reserved.

Scripture quotations noted RSV are from the Revised Standard Version of the Bible. Copyright © 1946, 1952, 1971, 1973, by the Division of Christian Education of the National Council of the Churches of Christ in the U.S.A. Used by permission.

Scripture quotations noted THE MESSAGE are from *The Message.* Copyright © 1993, 1994, 1995, 1996, 2000, 2001, 2002. Used by permission of NavPress Publishing Group.

Scripture quotations noted TLB are from *The Living Bible,* copyright © 1971. Used by permission of Tyndale House Publishers, Inc., Wheaton, Illinois 60189. All rights reserved.

FaithWords
Hachette Book Group
237 Park Avenue
New York, NY 10017

Visit our Web site at www.faithwords.com.

Printed in the United States of America

First Edition: February 2009
10 9 8 7 6 5 4 3 2 1

FaithWords is a division of Hachette Book Group, Inc.
The FaithWords name and logo are trademarks of Hachette Book Group, Inc.

Library of Congress Cataloging-in-Publication Data

McAllister, Dawson.
A walk with Christ to the cross : the last fourteen hours of His earthly mission / Dawson McAllister. — 1st ed.
p. cm.
ISBN-13: 978-0-446-19696-3
1. Jesus Christ—Passion. I. Title.
BT431.3.M37 2009
232.96—dc22
2008017651

I would like to dedicate this book to my late father,

Dr. Eugene McAllister,

for his modeling of the Christian life to me.

Contents

PART II
A CLOSER LOOK

Foreword

Nearly twenty years ago I met Dawson McAllister, who changed the direction of my life. I was a burnt-out, fourth-year college student in southern California. In addition to my studies, I was a member of a magic club in Beverly Hills and had begun doing magic shows for teenagers incorporating the truth of Jesus Christ.

I had grown up not taking ministry to teenagers very seriously, believing it was mainly about entertainment, keeping them off the streets and away from temptations.

But then I saw Dawson take a group of ten thousand students on the most detailed encounter of Christ's journey to the cross I had ever experienced. As a twenty-one-year-old who had grown up in the church and studied the Bible on a collegiate level, I was refreshed and revived. New hope for others and myself filled my life. Dawson had reconnected me to the story of Christ's brutal crucifixion I had heard hundreds of times.

I was transformed, not only by the message of the cross that I had taken for granted, but also at what I saw happen in the lives of the teenagers present. They were still, quiet, and focused as Dawson shared with them for nearly seven hours. And in a room of ten thousand, it was rare to see a student get up to go to the bathroom or lean over to a friend to whisper! These students were spellbound, captivated by the one story that changes everything about life. I realized I had heard the story so many times, I had forgotten to live in its power.

As Jesus had called His disciples, Dawson then asked me to follow him, joining the powerful ministry to teenagers he was leading. I left everything I had been doing and joined his conference ministry. The message of the cross compels us to lose our lives, knowing that only then can we find them.

So take a walk with Christ to the cross. Whether it is your first time or one of many, I pray your life is never the same again.

— Mark Matlock

President, WisdomWorks Ministries, Irving, Texas

Acknowledgments

Thanks to Dan Vorm for his work putting this material into book form, to Gary Terashita for envisioning this project and bringing it to fruition, and to Holly Halverson, for her fine editing work along the way.

Also, thanks to the entire staff of the Dawson McAllister Association for their encouragement, hard work, and support.

A WALK WITH CHRIST TO THE CROSS

PART I

STEP-BY-STEP

If I had a time machine, there are many points in history I'd love to visit. Perhaps I'd travel back to famous battles of the Civil War or sit in Yankee Stadium watching Babe Ruth hit a home run. I'd love to hear the sound of George Washington's voice as he crossed the Delaware, or I might even peek in on my parents when they were children.

Without a doubt, however, there's one slice of world history I'd want to see above all the rest. I would love to have observed Jesus Christ as He walked this earth two thousand years ago—to hear the love in His voice as He approached common people, and His righteous anger when confronting the sin of the Jewish leaders. To watch Him heal the sick and turn water into wine. And most of all, to see the courage and determination in His eyes as He laid down His life for the sake of humankind.

Thankfully, I don't need time travel in order to learn of Jesus' life and ministry. God has recorded many details of

Christ's life in His precious Word, the Bible. Through the eyes of four of Jesus' faithful followers—Matthew, Mark, Luke, and John—we have the privilege of watching Jesus complete the most important mission in all of history: His determined walk to the Cross.

Come with me, then, as we explore the last fourteen hours of Jesus' earthly mission. Step-by-step, it will be a journey that will change our lives forever.

I

The Betrayer Unmasked

Thursday, 6:00 p.m.–11:30 p.m.

What would you say if someone were to ask you, "What is the biggest heart-cry of the typical person today?" In my experience it's really very simple. The average person today is asking, "Does anybody really love me?" People have a deep longing to know that they are loved.

As Christians our answer to this question is pretty straightforward: "Yes, somebody loves you. God loves you very much!" Yet any cynical individual will then ask a second question: "Really? Prove it. How is it possible to know that God has any love for me whatsoever?"

That's a good question. How can we know that God loves us? And even if we're assured of His love, is it possible to know the extent of His love for you and me?

The greatest proof that God loves you is the fact that Jesus Christ came to this earth to die for you. He loves you so much that it cost Him great pain and sacrifice. The Bible says, "Greater love has no man than this, that a man lay down his life for his friends" (John 15:13 RSV). It also tells us, "God demonstrates His own love toward us, in that while we were yet sinners, Christ died for us" (Rom. 5:8 NASB).

We're going to start our walk with Christ to the Cross by sitting with Jesus at the Last Supper. We'll then walk closely alongside Him during the last fourteen hours of His life, step-by-step, all the way until His final cry, "It is finished."

IT'S HARD TO DIE

There are a lot of reasons why Jesus Christ came to this earth, but I'll tell you the main reason—He came to die. To be honest, it's hard to die. By the time you read from here to the end of this chapter, a number of individuals across the nation will have tried to commit suicide. Statistics show, however, that for every completed suicide there are approximately one hundred unsuccessful attempts. You know why? Because it's hard to die.

I used to work in the psychiatric ward of a hospital and students would often approach me to show the scars on their arms. They'd say, "Dawson, I tried to kill myself." I would tell them, "No, you were just trying to get attention—there are better ways of killing yourself than by slitting your wrists."

We had one man in the psych ward who tried to kill himself twice. The first time he drank Drano, the liquid drain opener. Take my advice—do not drink Drano! (It takes away bad breath; actually, it takes away all breath.) He didn't die, but the doctors were forced to remove his esophagus and two-thirds of his stomach, as well as most of his vocal cords. It was not a pretty sight.

For the next several months we had to feed him by way of a tube that went directly into his stomach. He could no longer swallow his food. After many months of shock treatments and therapy he was sent home. Unfortunately, less than a year later I heard he'd tried to kill himself again, this time by holding a shotgun under his chin and pulling the trigger. But as he pulled the trigger something inside him said, "I want to live!" This caused him to jerk the gun forward as it exploded, blowing off the front of his face.

Once again he was with us in the psych ward. His nose was now pretty well gone, his sinuses were destroyed, and just a flap of skin covered what used to be his nostrils. One day as we were draining his sinuses and putting some gravy stuff into his stomach, he looked up at me and whispered with his hoarse voice, "I wanna die—I wanna die." You know what? I believed him. He'd certainly done his best to make it happen.

What amazed me was that deep within his soul, even as he was pulling that trigger, something inside him said, "Live!" You know why? Because it's hard to die.

How easy was it for Jesus Christ to die? Not easy at all.

The Bible says that Jesus is the source of life—all life has come from Him. Can you imagine, then, that the Person from whom all life originated was born to die?

Yet He didn't just die a normal death; His suffering was beyond description. Think about this fact: if you were to add up all the sufferings of humankind for all of eternity, they would not equal the amount of suffering Jesus experienced as He hung on the cross. Now that's mind-blowing!

Yes, Jesus came to die, but it wasn't easy. In fact, the closer He came to the moment of His death, the more distressed and troubled He became. Finally, that moment arrived during the feast of the Passover.

THE GOD WHO PASSES OVER

It was during these last days of Jesus' life that the Jews were celebrating the Passover feast in Jerusalem. You may or may not know much about the Passover, so let me explain. It's important to understand the significance of this feast to the history of Israel. In fact, the last meal that Jesus shared with His disciples was the Passover meal. So, what's this Passover all about?

Early in Israel's history God spoke to His prophet Moses while on the back side of the Arabian Desert. God said, "Moses." Moses said, "What?" (I'm paraphrasing here.) God said, "Go and tell Pharaoh to let My people go." You may remember that God's people, the Israelites, were slaves to the Egyptians at the time, and the pharaoh was their king.

So Moses said to Pharaoh, "Hey, Pharaoh, God says to let His people go!" Pharaoh's response? "Forget you, buddy."

So God said to Pharaoh, "Hey, Pharaoh, are you into frogs? Lots and lots of frogs?" So yea, verily, verily, there were frogs throughout the land.

Moses went back to Pharaoh a second time, but again the Egyptian king refused. Then God said, "Hey, Pharaoh, are you into grasshoppers?" So there were lots and lots of grasshoppers all throughout Egypt.

This is how it went, plague after plague, until finally God said to Moses, "Okay, this is what I'm going to do. I'm going to send My angel of death all throughout Egypt, and I'm going to kill the firstborn of every family." Can you imagine? That would be tragic, wouldn't it?

But God wasn't done speaking. "Now this is what I want you to tell every Israelite family," He continued. "Tell them to take a lamb and slay it, then take its blood and put it on the doorframe. And when I send My angel of death throughout all of Egypt, when the angel sees that blood, he will pass over your home without harming your child."

That evening it happened just as God said. The next morning wailing was heard throughout the land of Egypt. Even Pharaoh lost his firstborn son; he finally got a clue, and he let God's people go.

I'm sure you know the story from here. The Israelites left Egypt and headed out into the desert, but Pharaoh soon changed his mind and sent his Egyptian marines in hot pursuit. God opened the Red Sea to allow His people across, and then closed it on the Egyptians as they gave chase. Every one of the pursuers was drowned. (I guess you could say those Egyptians all became Baptists on that day!)

So what's the significance of the Passover? You see, when the angel of death came over the land, God didn't ask people, "Hey, are you good-looking? Are you smart? Are you wise?" He didn't ask any of those things. Do you know what He was looking for? The blood. That's all He wanted to see—the blood of a spotless lamb painted on each doorframe.

The Bible tells us that Jesus Christ is our Passover. What does that mean? When you and I someday stand before God in judgment, He's not going to look at us and say, "Hey, were you good-looking? Were you rich? Were you a pom-pom girl or a football star? Did you have a successful life in the world's eyes?"

No, He's not going to ask any of those things. Do you know what He's going to say? He'll say, "Was the blood of Christ over you?" In other words, have you trusted Christ for His forgiveness, allowing His death to pay the penalty for your sins? If this is true of you, the Bible says you are no longer under judgment, for Christ was judged in your place. In this way Christ is our Passover—His judgment will pass over you.

THE ONE WHO WOULD BETRAY

Now we go to the Upper Room and Jesus' last meal with His disciples. He first washed their feet and then taught them many things during supper. The Bible says,

> After Jesus had said these things and while they were still reclining at the table and eating, He became deeply troubled and said, "I'm telling you the truth: One of you will betray Me, even someone who is eating with Me!" The disciples became extremely distressed and looked around at each other, wondering who He meant. They began to ask each other which one of them might do this. One by one they asked Him, "Lord, am I the one?" (Matt. 26:21–22; Mark 14:18–19; Luke 22:23; John 13:21–22 TGL, p. 220)

In order to get the correct picture in our minds, we must understand that in those days people reclined at a table on pillows instead of sitting on chairs. Maybe you've heard the old joke about this event. Question: "What were Christ's last words at the Last Supper?" Answer: "All of you who want to get in the picture get on this side of the table."

Basically, what they had here was a table that was U-shaped. They would lean on the table with one elbow and then use the opposite hand for eating. As a person ate he would have one person next to him and another person behind him. That's why the Bible says that John was "leaning back on Jesus' breast" (John 13:25 NKJV). This makes us believe that John was seated next to Jesus that evening, with Judas on Jesus' other side, or at least very close to Him.

So there they are, eating the Passover meal and listening to Jesus' last-minute instructions, when something awful happens. Christ has already been sorrowful during that entire week, but now it's the night before the Crucifixion, and He becomes extremely sorrowful.

The passage tells us that Jesus became "deeply troubled." Do you know what that means? The Greek word translated "troubled in spirit" is a phrase used by those who work with horses. I don't know if you're into horses, but I am. When a horse gets agitated and gives a peculiar shudder and a snort, you'd better get out of the way—the horse is upset. The Bible says that Jesus uttered this same kind of guttural, painful groan—He was very, very troubled.

Christ's whole expression and the tone of His voice must have changed dramatically. Something awful grabbed hold of Christ's spirit and shook Him deep within, causing Him intense mental, emotional and spiritual pain. Jesus was announcing that one of His own, who would later be revealed as Judas Iscariot, was going to betray Him. Working with Satan, this tragic figure of history—in an act of cruelty, cowardice, and hard-heartedness—would hand Jesus over to His murderous enemies.

Why was Jesus so troubled in spirit at the thought of Judas' betrayal? To help answer this question, let's look at two prophecies that predicted the Messiah's betrayal at the hand of a friend. Both come from the Psalms, where the words and experiences of King David foreshadow the suffering of the Christ. In Psalm 41:9 David was saddened over the fact that "even my close friend, whom I trusted, he who shared my bread, has lifted up his heel against me" (NIV). And again, in Psalm 55:12–14, David wrote,

> If an enemy were insulting me,
> I could endure it;
> if a foe were raising himself against me,
> I could hide from him.
> But it is you, a man like myself,
> my companion, my close friend,
> with whom I once enjoyed sweet fellowship
> as we walked with the throng at the house of God. (NIV)

Jesus knew these psalms, and surely they were in His mind as He experienced the betrayal of His close friend and follower, Judas.

Then Jesus announced, "I'm telling you the truth: One of you will betray Me, even someone who is eating with Me!" This was hard for Jesus, because He then had to reveal the betrayer as Judas Iscariot, a person He cared for very much. I have a couple of boys, both of whom I've adopted. I love them so much I would die for them. But remember this: Jesus loved Judas a million times more than you and I have ever loved anybody. He was upset that someone He loved so much was going to betray Him. No wonder He was troubled.

As for the rest of the disciples, this talk of a betrayer must have hit them like a ton of bricks. The Bible says a hushed silence came over the room, then each of them began to look around in order to see who it might be. Who had a guilty look about him? Was it Matthew? Was it John? Their eyes bounced from man to man. Was it Peter? The person Jesus was talking about was at the table—it was one of them—but they couldn't figure it out.

They even got into small groups, and in these groups they had discussions. "Who is the betrayer?" they wondered together. Still, they couldn't figure out the answer. After some time, they finally approached Christ one by one, saying, "Lord, is it I?"

Let me ask you a question at this point in the story. If you had been in the room that night, what would've come to your mind? What weakness in your life might have caused a shadow of guilt to fall over you, perhaps prompting you to ask the question, "Lord, is it I?" Every one of us should ask ourselves this question.

But now back to the story.

> He said to them, "It is one of the twelve, one who is dipping his hand in the dish with Me. Look, the

> hand of the one who is betraying Me is with Me on the table. The Son of Man will indeed go as it has been determined and predicted in the Scriptures. But how awful it will be for the one who betrays Him! It would have been better for that man if he had never been born." (Matt. 26:23–24; Mark 14:20–21; Luke 22:21–22 TGL, p. 221)

Ah, now Judas "how-could-you-do-this" Iscariot has just figured out that Jesus knows what he knows. Always an actor, Judas himself leans over to Christ and says, "Rabbi, am I the one?" (Matt. 26:25 TGL, p. 221). And Jesus replies, "You have said it yourself" (26:25 TGL, p. 221), which is Greek slang for our modern phrase "Right on, buddy," or, "You've got that right."

THE BETRAYER UNMASKED

Who is this man Judas Iscariot? How could someone live with Jesus Christ for three long years, then turn against Him? Judas spent time with the greatest teacher who ever taught, the greatest preacher who ever preached, and the greatest healer who ever healed. Jesus was the most fantastic man in all of history. How, then, could Judas now betray the Son of God?

The mystery of Judas Iscariot has been called the darkest mystery in the Bible. The Scriptures don't reveal much about Judas's background. He must have had some great potential, some unique qualities that Jesus saw in him. As a result, Jesus gave Judas the most honored opportunity of all—the privilege of walking with Him personally.

From the Scriptures we know that Judas . . .

- Knew Christ face-to-face.
- Walked with Christ every day.
- Heard most of what Christ taught.
- Witnessed most of what Christ accomplished.
- Was trained to be an apostle by Christ Himself.
- Served on witnessing tours under Christ's personal command.
- Was a leader among the disciples, and was respected by them.
- Was an outstanding business leader.
- Was the treasurer of the group.
- Enjoyed the love and camaraderie of his fellow disciples.
- Was warned of sin's consequences by Christ Himself.

There's much to be said for the strengths and opportunities Judas had been given. He had the potential and rare opportunity for real greatness. Yet he fell to the depths of evil. Why? What fatal flaws caused him to turn his back on Jesus Christ? There are at least two made clear in Scripture.

JUDAS AND SELFISH AMBITION

First, it would appear Judas had the flaw of selfish ambition. Evidently he joined up with Christ for all the wrong reasons. Like many Jews of his day, Judas had a basic misunderstanding regarding the Messiah. He thought Christ was going to trample all religious and political obstacles and set up a kingdom on this earth. Judas had great hopes for Jesus, expecting Him to gather a huge following that would ignore the religious leaders and free Israel from the iron rule of Rome. Perhaps he even told himself that once the kingdom was in place, Judas himself would become Christ's prime minister. He followed Jesus out of selfish ambition instead of humbly serving Christ as the true and living God!

At first, it appears some of Judas's expectations were being met. Crowds began to follow Jesus, hoping He would declare Himself the Messiah. And Jesus performed great miracles and preached powerful sermons. All the while, the religious leaders seemed powerless to stop Him. Judas must have said to himself, *Yes, this is the man. When He hits it big, I'll be right there with Him.*

I met a man a few years ago who was a store manager for a guy named Sam Walton. One day Sam told him, "I'm going to start a bunch of stores, and you'd be wise to buy as much stock in this company as you can." So this guy begged and borrowed until he had $50,000 to invest.

Today, of course, we recognize these stores by the name Wal-Mart. This man, who is now worth $700 million, was in the right spot at the right time, and he made the best of it. Maybe this is how Judas viewed his relationship with Jesus. He couldn't wait until Jesus took the Roman Empire by force—he would be right there with Him!

Over time, though, Christ's ministry began to change, and Judas didn't like what he saw. For example, Jesus would say things that offended His large following. He didn't tell the crowds what they wanted to hear, but instead spoke things that made them uncomfortable. And rather than amassing an army to fight the Romans, Jesus spent His days with the poor and the sick—even tax collectors and the least influential members of society. This must have grated on Judas's nerves.

Beyond all this, Jesus made it clear that His kingdom was not of this world. He even talked of His quickly approaching death at the hands of His enemies. Obviously, this was not going as Judas had planned, and he became increasingly bitter; Jesus was not the Messiah he had hoped for. Not at all.

THE POINT OF TURNING

You may say, "Dawson, can you pinpoint the moment when Judas turned against Christ?" I believe I can; it was approximately one year before the Crucifixion. Jesus had just fed five thousand men with five small loaves of bread and two fishes. The following day Jesus crossed to the other side of the Sea of Galilee to rest. When the crowd realized Jesus was gone, they got into boats and went to Capernaum to find Him. It must have been an amazing sight—hundreds of boats arriving on the far shore, coming to see Christ. Perhaps Judas saw this as the moment when Jesus would announce the establishment of His earthly kingdom.

Instead, Jesus not only offended the crowds but also infuriated them by His words and actions. He even scolded them for their wrong fleshly motives. Instead of endearing Himself to those who wanted to make Him king, He taught things that were difficult to understand. They wanted a Messiah who would lead them to overthrow Rome. When Jesus refused to fit their mold most of them turned away, wanting nothing to do with Him. This must have infuriated Judas. It's my belief that this was the day, after nearly two years of following Christ, Judas aligned with the crowds and became bitter toward Jesus. His heart began to turn against his Master.

If that's true, why did Judas continue as one of Christ's disciples? Perhaps he believed he could still force Jesus toward a political agenda. Or maybe he was already scheming about how he might betray Him. It could be he felt trapped, not knowing how to walk away from it all. Whatever the reason, I'm sure he felt he'd wasted two years on a dream that was now dashed to pieces.

JUDAS AND HIS GREED

Not only was Judas flawed by selfish ambition, but he also possessed an unquenchable desire for money. He had the fatal flaw of greed. The story of Jesus and Mary at Bethany tells of Judas's greed and his embezzlement of the disciples' money:

> Six days before the Passover, Jesus arrived at Bethany, where Lazarus lived, whom Jesus had raised from the dead. Here a dinner was given in Jesus' honor. Martha served, while Lazarus was among those reclining at the table with him. Then Mary took about a pint of pure nard, an expensive perfume; she poured it on Jesus' feet and wiped his feet with her hair. And the house was filled with the fragrance of the perfume. But one of his disciples, Judas Iscariot, who was later to betray him, objected, "Why wasn't this perfume sold and the money given to the poor? It was worth a year's wages." He did not say this because he cared about the poor but because he was a thief; as keeper of the money bag, he used to help himself to what was put into it. (John 12:1–6 NIV)

Ah, Judas. Now it's clear what motivated him at the core. Did he care about people? Did he even care about his Master, Jesus, who was telling the disciples about His impending death? Not at all. Judas cared about no one but himself, as evidenced by his selfish ambition and his lust for personal gain.

Soon after the event with the perfume, Judas decided to strike a deal with Jesus' enemies, the Jewish leaders. His anger had reached a boiling point, and he was now ready to help those who wanted Jesus destroyed. The leaders needed Judas's help in identifying Jesus. They could recognize Christ during the day, but were afraid to arrest Him in daylight for fear it would cause a riot. They wanted to find Him under the cover of night, but they were afraid they would not be able to identify Jesus in the darkness.

Judas, with his inside knowledge of Christ's whereabouts, became valuable to the religious leaders. He knew where Christ was at all times, and could easily point Him out in the darkness. Needless to say, the leaders must have been very pleased when bitter Judas came to them and offered his services. In Matthew 26:14–16 we're told: "Then one of the twelve, named Judas Iscariot, went to the chief priests and said, 'What are you willing to give me to betray Him to you?' And they weighed out thirty pieces of silver to him. From then on he began looking for a good opportunity to betray Jesus" (NASB).

THE MOMENT OF DECISION

And so, eating with Christ and the disciples at the Last Supper, the simmering bitterness and greed of Judas

Iscariot came to a head. Events were happening quickly, and Judas felt the pressure to act. When John asked Jesus to reveal the betrayer's identity, Christ did so by practicing a familiar custom. He took a cracker or piece of bread and dipped it into a sauce that was on the table. He then offered it to Judas. This was a Jewish custom, a means of offering friendship. Remarkably, it appears that Christ was offering Judas one more chance to repent of his evil plan and commit himself to his Master.

For a few brief seconds Judas stood on the brink of life and death, heaven and hell. Yet he stayed with his earlier decision to turn against Jesus, and in doing so rejected His offer of love. Immediately, Satan himself entered into Judas. Knowing this, Jesus commanded Judas, "What you are about to do, do quickly" (John 13:27 NIV). That is to say, *I know your plans with the Jewish leaders, so I command you to get on with it!*

The drama in the Upper Room had reached its conclusion. Judas left the room and headed into the darkness to perform his horrendous crime. The other disciples were confused about what was taking place, never suspecting what Judas had in mind. Jesus, however, knew His steps toward the Cross were now quickening.

LESSONS TO LEARN

The story of Judas Iscariot tells us much we can apply to our own lives. It's possible to be . . .

- Loved by Jesus
- Gifted
- Around other Christians
- Students of the teachings of Christ
- A "supposed" Christian leader
- One who witnesses supernatural miracles
- Respected by others

. . . and still be an enemy of Christ. Unless we turn from our fatal flaws (sin) and believe Christ for who He is (Lord and Savior), it's possible we too might find ourselves disappointed in the message of the Cross. As with Judas, this can only lead to eternal tragedy.

2

Peter Will Be "Sifted"

Have you ever wondered what it was like to be one of Jesus' disciples? It would have been a tremendous privilege to live alongside the Messiah. He is the Hope of the Ages, the Son of God—how fascinating to watch His every move, to hang on His every word. Yet there was a cost involved as well, for with great privilege comes great responsibility. The disciples often found themselves in the eye of the storm, witnessing spiritual battles that would determine the very destiny of humankind. Thus, we see these men at their best and their worst as they struggle to live out their faith in the midst of great conflict.

Of all the personalities revealed in the pages of the New Testament, Peter, the burly fisherman, is one of the most colorful. No one can read the story of Jesus without being drawn to Peter; marveling at his boldness, yet cringing at his failures. Peter's rough-hewn determination to follow Jesus, combined with the pitfalls of his human frailty, provide a stark backdrop for Jesus' walk to the Cross. Peter's impulsive, often reckless actions disclose a heart that's immature yet childlike in its love for the Savior. His dramatic story helps us understand the events leading to the Crucifixion. It also gives us a glimpse within ourselves. There's much for us to learn from Peter's remarkable story.

Who was this boisterous follower of Jesus named Peter? Like Jesus, he was a native of Galilee, a region in northern Israel. Galileans had an accent that was easily recognized by people in other parts of Israel, and were considered "lower class" than those in other regions. We also know Peter was a fisherman by trade, along with his brother Andrew and their partners, James and John. Initially, Peter and Andrew were disciples of John the Baptist. They became disciples of Jesus, however, when John revealed Jesus as "the Lamb of God who takes away the sin of the world!" (John 1:29 NASB).

Peter was part of Jesus' inner circle, which also included James and John. He was the first disciple to confess that Jesus is the Christ, the Son of the living God (see Matt. 16:16), and the only disciple allowed by Christ to walk on water. He also was a witness to the Transfiguration, where Jesus revealed His glory as He conversed with Moses and Elijah. Peter experienced and witnessed many amazing things, yet was known to be quick-tempered, impulsive, argumentative, and slow to grasp the teachings of Christ. Unfortunately, he became famous for his three denials of Christ before the Crucifixion, yet Christ forgave him and made him a key leader of the early church.

What an amazing life Peter lived. There are positive things we can learn from his example, and negative things he can teach us to avoid. So let's examine together the life of Peter, starting just after the Last Supper.

UNHEEDED WARNINGS

> When they had sung a hymn, they went out to the Mount of Olives. Then Jesus told them, "This very night you will all fall away on account of me, for it is written: 'I will strike the shepherd, and the sheep of the flock will be scattered.' But after I have risen, I will go ahead of you into Galilee." . . . Peter replied, "Even if all fall away on account of you, I never will." (Matt. 26:30–33 NIV)

Jesus responded with a warning:

> "Simon, Simon, Satan has asked to sift you as wheat. But I have prayed for you, Simon, that your faith may not fail. And when you have turned back, strengthen your brothers." But he replied, "Lord, I am ready to go with you to prison and to death." Jesus answered, "I tell you, Peter, before

> the rooster crows today, you will deny three times that you know me." (Luke 22:31–34 NIV)

> But Peter declared, "Even if I have to die with you, I will never disown you." And all the other disciples said the same. (Matt. 26:35 NIV)

It must have been late in the evening, somewhere near eleven o'clock, when Jesus and His eleven disciples made their way toward the Garden of Gethsemane on the Mount of Olives. As they passed through the Kidron Valley, Jesus interrupted the deafening silence with an alarming prediction of His earnest disciples' soon-coming failures.

This must have been devastating. "Then Jesus told them, 'This very night you will all fall away on account of me, for it is written: "I will strike the shepherd, and the sheep of the flock will be scattered"'" (Matt. 26:31 NIV). How shocked and saddened they must have been. Yet Jesus delivered this stunning message to their hearts and minds with incredible authority. Certainly they'd heard Him speak with this kind of authority before, and they knew He meant what He said: "This very night you will all fall away on account of me."

Imagine hearing those words from Jesus. How scary, how very humbling for each of these men. The Greek word for "fall away" is *skandalizo,* from which we get our English word *scandal.*[1] It literally means "to set a trap," or "to place a stumbling block." Jesus was telling His men that later that night they were going to fall into a trap. They were going to "stumble over" what would soon happen to Jesus. The events that lay ahead would overwhelm them, causing them to desert their Master. Not one of them would stay true to Jesus over the next few hours.

Why did this happen? Why were they soon to be disloyal to Jesus? Apparently the disciples hadn't understood Jesus' warnings concerning His arrest, death, and resurrection. Though they heard His words, they simply couldn't imagine such things happening to the Messiah. Jesus knew that in just a few hours these men would face a stark reality; their dreams concerning Him would be dashed. It would be a stumbling block, indeed.

One commentator puts it this way:

> When Christ was arrested, the apostles questioned and wondered if Christ was really the Messiah. He did not resist arrest, and He did not use His mighty power. He was not leading the people in an uprising against the Romans, nor was He freeing Israel and setting up the nation as the center of God's kingdom. The apostles were disillusioned and perplexed; they simply could not understand. Their hopes were hanging upon a cross of despair.[2]

THE COMING SATANIC ATTACK

Peter didn't take Christ's words lightly. He must have thought to himself, *Doesn't Jesus know that I am depend-*

able, even to the end? So he replied, "Even if all fall away on account of you, I never will" (Matt. 26:33 NIV). But Jesus graciously told him, "Simon, Simon, Satan has asked to sift you as wheat" (Luke 22:31 NIV).

Obviously, Peter didn't grasp the seriousness of Christ's prediction. He didn't understand the forces of evil that would influence him and the others to fall away. Jesus, though, had made it clear: Satan himself was out to completely destroy Peter.

In the Bible, the repetition of a name is used to show deep emotion, heartfelt anxiety, and intense concern. We see this as Jesus deals with people throughout His ministry. In this instance He was showing deep emotion and concern over the trap Satan was setting for Peter and the others. Jesus was intensely concerned; He knew there was much more taking place in the spiritual realm than Peter could possibly understand. Therefore, Jesus pulled back the spiritual veil, just a bit, allowing His men to see the battle raging in the heavenly places.

We learn a number of things from this phrase, "Satan has asked to sift you as wheat." First, Satan is not allowed to tempt any believer at will. He can do so only with direct permission from God. Just as with Job (see the Old Testament book of that name), Satan had to receive permission from God to tempt Peter and his friends.

If God allows temptation, however, it doesn't give us permission to yield to that temptation. The Bible teaches that God will not abandon us, leaving us at the mercy of our attacker. We're told in 1 Corinthians 10:13, "No temptation has seized you except what is common to man. And God is faithful; he will not let you be tempted beyond what you can bear. But when you are tempted, he will also provide a way out so that you can stand up under it" (NIV).

Second, Satan desired to "sift" the disciples as wheat. What does this mean? In our mechanized society we may scratch our heads at this phrase; to the disciples, however, it made perfect sense. The process of sifting wheat was the separating, or filtering, of the good (wheat) from the bad (chaff). It was a means of purification. Women would place the wheat from the fields in a large screened holder, shaking it back and forth vigorously. Eventually, the chaff would filter through the screen, leaving behind the desired wheat.

I like the way John Piper describes this process, and how it applies to faith and temptation:

> We can imagine a picture like this: Satan has a big sieve with jagged edge wires forming a mesh, with holes shaped like faithless men and women. What he aims to do is throw people into this sieve and shake them around over these jagged edges until they are so torn and weak and desperate that they let go of their faith and fall through the sieve as faithless people, right into Satan's company. Faith cannot fall through the mesh. It is the wrong shape. And so as long as the disciples hold to their faith, trusting the power and the goodness of God

> for their hope, then they will not fall through the mesh into Satan's hands.[3]

Satan's plan for you and me is the same as it was for Peter and the disciples. He desires to strike at the heart of God by sifting us, God's children. How does he do this? He may challenge God to remove the "sense" of His presence and blessings from us as Christians. Or he may whisper in our ear that God has abandoned us as we experience trial after trial. Sometimes he'll even accuse us of loving God not for who He is, but because of the blessings we receive from Him. Satan will try to confuse us, accuse us, and separate us from God's truth any way he can. This is why believers are told, "Resist the devil and he will flee from you" (James 4:7 NASB).

LESSONS LEARNED

Just as Christ predicted, later that evening the disciples were sifted like wheat. On that fateful night the very presence of Jesus was torn away from them. He was going to die, and the disciples were left alone with their earthly dreams shattered. All of them failed, especially Peter, who not only deserted Jesus but later denied three times that he ever knew Him. Yet God, in His grace, drew each of them back to an even deeper faith in Himself.

As we have seen, there are certain warning signs that

occur prior to a spiritual failure. In this story, Christ personally warned Peter and the disciples they were in danger. He told them that a satanic trap would soon overwhelm them all. As Christians we must be alert to the spiritual traps that surround us in this world. As we pay attention to God through His Word and through prayer, He warns us of their existence and guides us step-by-step.

Even though we're told our "adversary the devil prowls around like a roaring lion, seeking someone to devour" (1 Pet. 5:8 ESV), we don't need to fear. God is faithful. He will not allow Satan to tempt us beyond what we can bear.

3

Jesus in Agony at Gethsemane

Thursday, 11:30 p.m.–Friday, 1:00 a.m.

What would you do if you knew you were going to enter the longest night in all of history? What if you knew you were going to face the cruelest death anyone has ever experienced on earth? What would you do?

As Jesus led His disciples away from the Upper Room toward the Garden of Gethsemane, He knew He was facing this very thing, yet He didn't become grouchy or angry. The Bible says Jesus did all things very well, for He was God. This proved true even in His suffering.

Matthew 26:36 says that Jesus went into the garden to pray: "Then Jesus went with His disciples across the Kidron Valley to a garden called Gethsemane. When they had entered the place, He said to them, 'Sit here while I go over there and pray'" (TGL, p. 237). If you were going through a terrible crisis in your life, and your friends didn't understand your pain, how would that make you feel toward them? One time a student came up to me and said, "Dawson, I want to talk with you." I told him he'd have to wait until I was done signing some books, and he agreed. It was a Saturday night, and he waited for an hour so we could talk.

When I was available he approached me and said, "I want to ask you one question: Why me?" I replied, "Why what?" He said, "My girlfriend just dropped me." I thought to myself, *Well, that happens. That's not a big deal.* Then he continued, "And the doctor just gave me eight months to live. I never did anything really, really bad. Why me?"

Imagine your doctor told you that same news, and when you went to your friends they just blew you off. How would you feel toward them? Jesus was about to experience something similar—His best friends were soon to abandon Him.

IN THE GARDEN

Did you know that Jesus was bankrolled by some very rich followers? Evidently one of them owned a large garden near Jerusalem, perhaps just inside the city limits. This garden had a large wall around it and was full of olive trees. It was a favorite place for Jesus, and He often went there to pray. "He took with Him Peter and the two sons of Zebedee, James and John, and began to be deeply grieved with great distress and agony. Then He said to them, 'My soul is extremely sorrowful even to the point of death. Stay here and watch with Me. Pray that you may not be tempted'" (Matt. 26:37–38; Mark 14:33–34; Luke 22:40b TGL, p. 237).

So Jesus took Peter, James, and John with Him farther into the garden, leaving the others at the entrance. It's at this point, as Jesus begins to pray, that something awful happens. The Bible says He began to be sorrowful and amazed and deeply distressed.

Let's take a look at these words, starting with the word *grieved.* Basically, it means that Christ almost went into shock! Jesus Christ saw or felt something so awful that His skin began to crawl and His hair stood on end. He was going into shock.

You say, "Dawson, what was that like?" I'm reminded of a buddy of mine who was a highway patrolman in Colorado. One evening he was called to the scene of a terrible accident. A young woman had driven off a mountain road and hit a tree or a rock; she was killed immediately, decapitated from her nose up.

My friend was told to clean up the car, for her parents were coming to examine the scene. He went back to the car and took pieces of bone and flesh and hair and brain, then stuffed it all into a paper sack. He carried the sack fifteen feet from the car and buried it. He later told me he couldn't sleep or eat for three days. It was a horribly traumatic experience. Now magnify that sickening feeling a million times, and you still haven't described the sickness in the pit of Christ's stomach during these moments in the garden.

Perhaps you've heard the tragic story of the pastor who, while backing his car out of his driveway, accidentally ran over his two-year-old son who'd been playing nearby. Imagine how he felt as he rushed to his dead child, seeing the tire's tread marks on his boy's crushed skull. Magnify by a million times how this father felt, and you still wouldn't be close to the suffering Jesus experienced in the garden. The Bible says He went into shock.

We're also told that Jesus began to be sorrowful. Have you ever been to a funeral where you see people who can't cry anymore? It's not because they don't want to; it's because they can't. They've cried until they can't cry anymore—their emotions are absolutely shot, pulled right out of them. This must be similar to what Christ was experiencing—all of Christ's sorrow was pulled right out of Him.

The Bible says Jesus became deeply distressed, and He began to shudder all over. He said to Peter, James, and John, "Men, you've got to pray for Me . . . I think I'm going to die!" There are some who even say that Jesus Christ, at that moment, suffered a slight heart attack. We don't know for sure, but the symptoms He experienced make that a possibility. Still, Jesus continued to push through the suffering.

> Then He went a little farther away, about the distance of a stone's throw, knelt on the ground, and fell on His face. He prayed that, if it were possible,

> this time of agony might pass from Him. "Abba, Father," He said, "everything is possible for You. My Father, if it is possible, let this cup pass from Me. Yet do not do what I will but what You will." (Matt. 26:39; Mark 14:35–36; Luke 22:41–42 TGL, p. 237)

STILL DEEPER IN PRAYER

Jesus put on His prayer shawl and went farther away from His disciples—deeper into the garden—then drew the shawl over His head. Most Westerners are unaware of the Oriental style of prayer, which is how Jesus would have prayed. In line with Jewish tradition, He would have knelt down, pressing His forehead onto the ground. Those of us who are older will remember that Anwar Sadat (the former president of Egypt and a Muslim) had calluses on his forehead due to this manner of prayer. That's how people pray in the Middle East. Jesus literally fell on His face in great pain and suffering before the Father.

Lying on the ground, He began to pray that the hour might pass. He cried out, saying, "Abba, Father." Do you know what *Abba* means? It means "My dearest Daddy"! He continued, "All things are possible for You. Take this cup away from Me; nevertheless, not what I will, but what You will" (Mark 14:36 NKJV).

I believe that Jesus—at this moment—was making

His final decision about whether or not to go to the Cross. I know we're talking about mystery here, but Jesus was not simply a yo-yo on the Father's string. He made a true yes or no decision about going to His death. His humanity cried out "No!" for as a man He surely struggled with questions common to humankind. Could He do it? Did it seem right to have all our sin laid on Him at once? Could He bear the utter hell of being forsaken by God? Was humankind worth the suffering? These and other questions must have gone through Christ's mind. With heartbreak on His face He cried out, "Abba, Father! Is there another way?"

CHOOSING THE ONLY WAY

I was once in a school classroom lecturing about Jesus when a student stood up and said, "Come on, man . . . I'm Jewish. Am I going to hell because I'm Jewish?" I replied, "No, the greatest Jew who ever lived was Jesus Christ, the Messiah. No, you won't go to hell because you're Jewish. If you do go to hell, it's because you've rejected Him as your Savior."

He said, "Come on . . . you've got Buddha, you've got the Jewish way, all of these religions . . . all these different ways to God. How can you say that Jesus is the only way to God?" I responded, "Well, I didn't say it; Jesus said it for me."

In my opinion, he had a good question. How can we say that Jesus is the only way? It's such a good question, in fact, that Jesus asked that very thing while on His face in the garden. He said, "Father, is there another way?" The answer, of course, was no; Jesus' suffering, death, and resurrection were the only means by which we could have access to the Father.

After an intense struggle, Jesus came out from the depths of the garden and found His men sleeping.

> He said to Peter, "Simon, are you asleep? So you couldn't watch with Me for even one hour! Watch and pray that you may not be tempted. The spirit is willing but the flesh is weak."
>
> A second time He went off and prayed. "My Father," He said, "if You are willing, take away this cup from Me. Yet if this cannot pass from Me unless I drink it, do Your will and not My own."
>
> Then an angel from heaven appeared to Him and strengthened Him. He was in agony and prayed even more fervently, and His sweat became like large drops of blood falling to the ground. (Matt. 26:40–42; Mark 14:37–39; Luke 22:42–44 TGL, p. 237)

At this point Jesus went back into the garden a second time, now sweating bloody drops all over the rocks. He was experiencing a medical condition called "hematidrosis." Have you ever sweat? Of course. Have you ever bled? Yes. Have you ever sweat blood? No. But Jesus did, and it wasn't just a small trickle of blood coming from His forehead. The blood came from pores all over His body.

How did this happen—what caused it? This can happen when stress upon stress is laid over a person's emotions. Sometimes an individual will push out from within himself in incredible agony. If the person pushes hard enough, either he'll pass out cold or blood will pass through his veins until it hits the sweat glands. This is why Jesus, in such stress and agony, sweat great drops of blood.

THE AGONY OF HIS DECISION

You may say, "But Dawson, I don't understand the agony. He wasn't on the cross yet." Let me go back to a previous statement that may have sounded to you like heresy. I said that Jesus' human nature did not want to go to the Cross. Let's explore this further. Look at what the great prophet Isaiah predicted concerning the suffering of Christ on the cross:

> The Lord GOD has opened My ear;
> And I was not disobedient
> Nor did I turn back.
> I gave My back to those who strike Me,
> And My cheeks to those who pluck out the beard.
> (Isa. 50:5–6 NASB)

Let me stop here for a second. When Isaiah predicted that men would "pluck out the beard," he was saying that men would grab Christ by His beard and pull it out in chunks. Many don't know that when Jesus Christ hung on the cross He was no longer recognizable as a man. His face was wretched beyond recognition.

Isaiah's prediction continues:

> I did not cover My face from humiliation and
> spitting.
> For the Lord God helps Me,
> Therefore, I am not disgraced;
> Therefore, I have set My face like flint,
> And I know that I will not be ashamed.
> (Isa. 50:6–7 NASB)

Jesus set His face to do the Father's will—He set it like flint, which is the hardest rock there is. In other words, He was determined to do His Father's will at any cost.

Still, His humanity wanted to resist the suffering that lay ahead. For example, if somebody called me tonight and said, "Dawson, do you love Jesus?" I would say yes. Imagine if they then said, "Good, because we have one of your boys, and if you don't denounce Christ within the next three hours we're going to kill him." On one hand I would want to do the Father's will and not denounce Christ. On the other hand my whole system would be shouting, "NO!"

Do you get it? Jesus set His face to do the Father's will,

yet when He looked at the massive, incredible suffering ahead of Him, His humanity cried out, "NO!" In spite of His feelings, Christ set His face like flint. He battled the emotional pressure, and during the intensity of it all He sweat blood all over the rocks.

Perhaps Jesus would have died right there if the Father hadn't sent an angel to comfort Him. I don't know if the angel gave him food and water or just encouragement, but in some way the angel ministered to Jesus. Can you imagine? Here's Jesus, the almighty and powerful God who created everything—all things were made by Him—being ministered to by a created being, an angel. If we use our imaginations, we can see Christ with His face on the ground, covered with bloody sweat, saying, "Can somebody help Me? Could somebody please help Me?" God did help Him, by sending a comforting angel.

LESSONS TO LEARN

What can we learn from the Garden of Gethsemane? First, we learn about humility. Let's face it—if you and I had been walking by that garden and looked over the wall, we wouldn't have said, "Oh, I get it . . . God in human form! That must be God in the flesh." No, we would have seen a man in deep distress, falling down and getting up, falling down and getting up, crying out, "Abba, Father, My dearest Daddy, let this hour pass from Me." Our first reaction would have been, "Who is this peasant Jew having a nervous breakdown?"

Can you imagine what the angels in heaven must have been thinking? They must have been shocked at what was happening in the dust of Gethsemane. The Bible says Christ made Himself of no reputation. In the garden we see this firsthand.

The second thing we learn from Gethsemane is that sin is no small thing to Jesus Christ. What was it that He saw in the garden? We know it troubled Him deeply, even to the point of death. What was it that caused Him to shrink back in horror?

I believe He saw sin in all its fury. Maybe He saw all of the abused babies in the world; or perhaps he saw the more than two hundred thousand teenage mothers who abort their babies every year.[1] Perhaps He saw the effects of drunk teenage drivers. It could be that He saw what Hitler did. It's possible He saw how you and I have sinned, as well. Whatever it was, it almost killed Him.

The third thing we learn is this: Jesus considered us worth the suffering. I don't feel worthy of His sacrifice, but who am I to argue with Jesus? On that fateful night Jesus decided we were worth the cost; He determined to suffer that we might have peace with God for all eternity. In Hebrews 12:2 we're told to fix "our eyes on Jesus, the author and perfecter of faith, who for the joy set before Him endured the cross, despising the shame" (NASB). He despised the shame of the Cross so we might have peace with God.

Jesus loves you, and as difficult as it is to believe, Jesus made a decision about you in the Garden of Gethsemane. He decided you were worth dying for. Now here's the question He asks today: "Am I worth living for?"

This is a hard question. Please don't answer it lightly, for it costs to be a Christian. You say, "Dawson, if I truly follow Christ the way He wants me to, a lot of my friends won't understand." You're absolutely right. That's why I encourage you to think about this decision . . . weigh it . . . sweat over it, for He sweat great drops of blood in deciding about you.

A few years ago a girl approached me and said, "Dawson, I have a problem. I love my boyfriend, and I love God. But we've gone too far sexually—we've gone all the way."

I said, "Do you think your boyfriend is walking with God?" The obvious answer, of course, was no. Then I asked her if she thought her boyfriend was a Christian. She replied, "Well, he talks about God." I reminded her that Satan talks about God all the time—talking doesn't make one a Christian. I said, "Look, the Scripture is clear. Let me just say this very quickly: Drop him! The Bible says drop him!"

"But Dawson," she responded, "you don't understand. I really love my boyfriend." I told her again she needed to end the relationship, but she kept insisting she could love both him and God. Finally, I felt I needed to state the obvious: "Dear, let me rephrase what you're saying—you *like* God, and you *love* your boyfriend." At that, she lowered her head and walked away. I don't know what she did with the Lord on that decision, but I do know this: it wasn't going to be an easy choice.

Every person in the world faces this simple question: Is Jesus Christ worth living for? He's worth living for or He's not; you must decide for yourself. But as you decide, remember Jesus Christ in the garden—falling down, getting up, falling down, getting up. Then see Him, with His broken heart in extreme agony, as He looks directly in your eyes and says, "Yes, you're worth it."

4

The Pride and Prayerlessness of Peter

As we saw previously, Jesus in His love was preparing Peter and the disciples for the trials and heartbreak that lay ahead. He warned them they would desert Him that very night. Jesus spoke to them of Satan's desire to sift them as wheat, which is to say, Satan longed to destroy their faith. Peter, however, refused to be humbled and comforted by Christ's words. In fact, he was personally insulted by what Jesus said, and his heart rebelled against what he was hearing.

Peter was a prideful man, and this caused him to fail in many ways during the night ahead. His actions proved true the words found in Proverbs 16:18 (NIV): "Pride goes before destruction, a haughty spirit before a fall." Let's examine Peter's prideful attitude, and seek to learn from his mistakes.

A SUPERIOR ATTITUDE

Do you remember Jesus' warning to the disciples as they left the Upper Room? He quoted the Scriptures: "I will strike down the shepherd, and the sheep of the flock shall be scattered" (Matt. 26:31 NASB). But Peter replied, "Even if all fall away on account of you, I never will" (26:33 NIV). A little later he exclaimed, "Lord, I am ready to go with you to prison and to death" (Luke 22:33 NIV). Again, after Jesus told Peter he would deny Him three times that night, Peter declared, "Even if I have to die with you, I will never disown you" (Matt. 26:35 NIV). We admire Peter's love and zeal for the Savior, don't we? Yet he was wrong to show contempt for the other disciples by pridefully comparing himself to them. By doing this he revealed his attitude of superiority.

Peter set himself up for a terrible fall. He was offended and belligerent at Christ's words. In the original Greek, Matthew 26:33 reveals Peter's boast to be incredibly appalling. The pronoun "I" is emphatic, meaning it is heavily stressed. Peter was determined that Jesus recognize him as better than the others; they may fall away, but never him. In fact, Peter's answer to Christ would have been comical had it not been so sad. He said, in so many words, *Look, Jesus, I agree with You. These other disciples are not dependable, but You can count on me.*

One commentator puts it this way:

> Matthew, the former publican, might perhaps stoop down to that low moral level of abandoning the Master in His hour of affliction. "My former fishing partners, James and John, might also conceivably fall into this trap. In fact, I wouldn't even put it past my own brother Andrew . . . but not I." In reality he does not even say, "not," but "never" which is much stronger.[1]

Peter took it even further. He said, "Even if all fall away on account of you, I never will." Not only was he saying he was superior to the disciples, but to all men everywhere.

Ah, Peter. There is no question he was sincere as he boasted of his superior allegiance to Christ. Certainly, in his own heart, Peter could not comprehend that he would ever deny his Lord and Master. His pride was bolstered when he looked at the weaknesses of the other disciples and failed to look at his own. The Bible is clear, however, that nothing good happens when we arrogantly compare ourselves with others. The great preacher C. H. Spurgeon once said, "He who thinks himself so much stronger than his brethren, is the very man who will prove to be weaker than any of them, as did Peter, not many hours after his boast was uttered."[2]

AN ATTITUDE OF OVERCONFIDENCE

It's obvious from Peter's words that, like most of us, he didn't really know himself. He didn't grasp the weakness of his own soul. Nor did he understand the teachings of the Old Testament prophet Jeremiah, who said, "The heart is deceitful above all things, and desperately wicked; who can know it?" (Jer. 17:9 NKJV).

Perhaps we should ask why so few of us really know who we are and what we're capable of doing. Like Peter, we may have a false sense of ourselves that often leads to heartache, both in us and in the lives of others. King David recognized this when he prayed, "Search me, O God, and know my heart; test me and know my anxious thoughts. See if there is any offensive way in me, and lead me in the way everlasting" (Ps. 139:23–24 NIV). It's a wise person who thinks neither too high nor too low of himself. Peter lacked that ability, and his overconfidence got him into trouble.

Peter's pride indicated a deeper problem, however. He was apparently convinced that he had the power, in and of himself, to stand for Christ no matter what. He didn't understand the weakness of his own flesh, and in his pride he thought he was above serious sin. This self-confidence led him to minimize even the very words of Jesus. The Son of God had just told Peter he was going to fall. Peter's response? *No way, not me.*

Can you think of a time when you thought you were strong only to discover you were, in fact, very weak? Peter's failure came when he didn't realize his need to be totally dependent upon Christ for everything. I like what another commentator has said: "As with all men, his natural strength failed. The need for the Lord's strength, the presence of the Holy Spirit to conquer self and evil was the great lesson Peter had to learn. Very simply, he and the others had to learn to trust the strength of Jesus."[3]

Peter learned this lesson the hard way. Perhaps later he remembered what Jesus had taught the disciples about the source of their strength. One day while passing through a vineyard, Jesus pointed to the plants and said, "I am the vine; you are the branches. If a man remains in me and I in him, he will bear much fruit; apart from me you can do nothing" (John 15:5 NIV). For most of us, as with Peter, this takes a lifetime to learn.

LESSONS TO LEARN

Before we move on, let's allow some personal application. Peter refused to believe Jesus' clear warnings about how he would fail. What are some of Christ's teachings that you are prone to ignore? Some of us may be chasing the world and all it contains, while Jesus tells us we can't serve both God and money (see Luke 16:13). Some may put their confidence in how spiritual they appear before men, refusing to believe that God looks at the heart (see 1 Sam. 16:7). Or perhaps we refuse to believe that our sins are a serious matter before a holy God (see Mark 9:47).

Jesus' words to us are often direct and specific, as they were to Peter. Christ knew Peter's heart, and Peter would have done well to humble himself rather than attempt to prove Jesus wrong. Instead, Peter's pride and attitude of superiority were revealed, not only to the rest of the disciples, but to all men since as well. Zealous Peter learned the hard way, and his example stands as a warning to us all. "God opposes the proud but gives grace to the humble" (1 Pet. 5:5 NIV).

FAILURE TO WATCH AND PRAY

Though he was supremely confident in his love for Christ, Peter's great pride caused him to fail his Lord. There were, however, other warning signs that foretold Peter's disaster. One of those signs was his lack of commitment and unwillingness to "watch and pray."

> Then He said to them, "My soul is extremely sorrowful even to the point of death. Stay here and watch with Me. Pray that you may not be tempted." (Matt. 26:38; Mark 14:34; Luke 22:40b TGL, p. 237)

> He returned to the disciples and found them sleeping. He said to Peter, "Simon, are you asleep? So you couldn't watch with Me for even one hour! Watch and pray that you may not be tempted. The spirit is willing, but the flesh is weak." (Matt. 26:40–41; Mark 14:37–38 TGL, p. 237)

Imagine how heartbreaking this scene must have been. Jesus was now drawing near His most difficult hour. "Stay here and keep watch with Me," He told His friends, "and pray that you will not fall into temptation."

I've often wondered why Jesus took Peter, James, and John inside the garden with Him. Certainly He longed for their prayer support, for He understood something they didn't: in times of crisis nothing is more important than prayer. Earlier in His ministry He had taught them "at all times they ought to pray and not to lose heart" (Luke 18:1 NASB). If there was ever a time for Jesus to lose heart, it was here in the garden. Thus, He invited His closest friends to join Him during His intense trial. In His humanity, He didn't want to be alone. He needed their support.

John MacArthur wrote this about Christ's motives:

> He wanted to teach them further about facing strong temptation with confidence in God rather than in themselves. In light of their self-declared dependability the disciples need to learn the humility and poverty of spirit that is necessary before God can effectively use His people (see Matthew 5:3). He wanted Peter, James and John to be convinced and convicted of their foolish smugness and feelings of invincibility. And He wanted them, in turn, to teach their fellow disciples that lesson.[4]

HOW TO WATCH AND PRAY

Jesus' urgent command to His disciples was basic yet powerful. He commanded them to "keep watch . . . and pray." The word for "watch" in the original Greek means "to *abstain from sleep; to be vigilant, or to guard against danger.*"[5] Jesus commanded them to keep watch, to stay awake and be alert. He wanted them to see the temptation that was coming, and He asked them to pray that they might face it well. Soon they would be severely tempted to disbelieve Jesus, to abandon Him to His enemies. They would even be tempted to renounce they knew Him at all. They were in a desperate situation, yet they did not understand their weakness.

Then Christ left His (supposedly praying) band of disciples to seek the Father. Dramatically, on His face in prayer, He pleaded His case. After an intense hour of prayer like none the world has ever seen, Jesus returned to the disciples only to find them sleeping. "Could you men not keep watch with Me for one hour?" He asked Peter. "Watch and pray so that you will not fall into temptation. The spirit is willing, but the body is weak." Peter, James, and John had disobeyed Him and yielded to their desire for sleep. Although Jesus knew they would desert Him, still He was stunned by their shameless self-centeredness and spiritual immaturity.

We can hear the pain in Jesus' words, can't we? At His most critical moment, Jesus discovered His closest friends were asleep. He knew them better than they knew themselves; He knew their intentions, their foibles, and their mistakes. He even foretold the fact that they would let Him down. All of this, however, did little to ease the pain of their indifference. It was devastating to find them sleeping when they should have been supporting Him, and themselves, in prayer.

Perhaps Jesus remembered how King David's followers had supported David during his time of grief. David's son Absalom had committed treason and attempted to take the kingdom from his father. The Bible tells how David's supporters followed him out of Jerusalem, even near the spot where Christ was then praying: "But David continued up the Mount of Olives, weeping as he went; his head was covered and he was barefoot. All the people with him covered their heads too and were weeping as they went up" (2 Sam. 15:30 NIV). Surely, Jesus must have longed for this kind of support from His followers. He had none, and it must have broken His heart.

FLESH AND SPIRIT

Remarkably, in His kindness Jesus helped His disciples understand their inability to watch and pray. He said to His friends, "The spirit is willing, but the body is weak." He knew that in their spirits they desired to do what was right, yet they faced the weaknesses common to all humanity. Man, by his very nature, lacks the discipline and strength to live up to His highest desires.

God understands our dilemma. Although we disappoint Him, He remembers what we are like in our flesh—weak and frail. Listen to these words spoken concerning ancient Israel:

> Yet he was merciful;
> he forgave their iniquities
> and did not destroy them.
>
> Time after time he restrained his anger
> and did not stir up his full wrath.
> He remembered that they were but flesh,
> a passing breeze that does not return.
> (Ps. 78:38–39 NIV)
>
> As a father has compassion on his children,
> so the Lord has compassion on those who fear him;
> for he knows how we are formed,
> he remembers that we are dust.
> (Ps. 103:13–14 NIV)

Though we are accountable for our sin, we know that God is gracious to us in every way. Jesus was hurt and disappointed by the actions of these disciples, yet He kindly assured them He understood why they had failed Him. Jesus is a wonderful friend, indeed.

The story doesn't end there, however. Jesus goes to pray alone three times, and each time He comes back to find Peter, James, and John sleeping. They simply could not keep their eyes open. The Gospel writer Luke tells us they were sleeping because they were "exhausted from sorrow" (22:45 NIV). John MacArthur wrote, "In fairness, it should be noted that sleep is often a means of escape, and the disciples may have slept more out of frustration, confusion and depression than apathy."[6] Another person put it this way: "They were sleeping because of the emotional strain and distress of the evening. As Luke says, they slept because of sorrow, that is, sadness."[7]

Finally, the time for prayer in the garden was over. Jesus had spent it wisely, in a disciplined and meaningful way. He prepared Himself for the onslaught of evil and suffering He would soon face. Peter, James, and John, on the other hand, spent their time sleeping. They were confident their own strength and devotion to Jesus would see them through. Is it any wonder that Jesus stood firm through His terrible ordeal of the Cross, while Peter and the others fell in disgrace?

5

An Awestruck Crowd

Friday, 1:00 a.m.–1:30 a.m.

Judas had been busy since leaving the Upper Room earlier that evening. Evidently he'd gone to Caiaphas, the high priest, to tell him of the opportunity to arrest Christ that night. Caiaphas gathered some temple police and then sought permission to use the services of a cohort of Roman soldiers. Once this band of men had been assembled, Judas led them to the garden.

> A large crowd approached while he was still speaking. The man named Judas, one of the twelve, was leading them. Judas also knew the place because Jesus had often gone there with His disciples. So Judas came there, accompanied by a cohort of soldiers, officers from the chief priests, Pharisees, teachers of the law, and the elders of the people, all bearing torches and lanterns and swords and clubs.

> The betrayer had given them a signal. He told them, "It's the one I kiss. Seize Him and lead Him safely away." As soon as he arrived, he approached Jesus to kiss Him. "My friend," Jesus said to him, "why have you come?" "Greetings, Master!" Judas said. And he kissed Him. "Judas," Jesus said, "do you betray the Son of Man with a kiss?" (Matt. 26:47–50a; Mark 14:43–45; Luke 22:47–48; John 18:2–3 TGL, p. 238)

THE ARREST IN THE GARDEN

If we had been at the garden, we'd have been awestruck at this large crowd making its way toward Jesus. Some scholars believe that between six hundred and a thousand men came swarming toward Christ, most of them Roman soldiers. Judas had committed himself to pointing out Christ to the Jewish leaders, who were hoping to arrest Him.

As Judas drew near, Jesus said, "Friend, for what purpose have you come?" Judas cried out, "Master, Master, greetings, Master!" He then kissed Jesus Oriental-style, which means on the side of both cheeks. Jesus responded with these words to His friend: "Judas, are you betraying the Son of Man with a kiss?" In short, *Judas, how can you do this?* Evidently, these words rang in Judas's heart all night long—*Judas, how could you betray the Son of Man with a kiss?*

The Bible tells us in John 18 that Jesus then stepped aside, away from Judas, and approached the crowd that had come to arrest Him. "Jesus knew everything that was about to happen to Him. He stepped forward and said to them, 'Who do you want?' 'Jesus of Nazareth!' they answered. Jesus replied, 'I AM.' Judas, the man betraying Him, was standing with them. When Jesus said, 'I AM,' they all drew back and fell to the ground" (vv. 4–6 TGL, p. 238).

Imagine! He says two simple words and *boom,* down they go!

To the Jews of that day, the phrase "I AM" meant one thing—"I AM GOD!" Thousands of years earlier, when God had met Moses in the desert and ordered him back to Egypt to lead the children of Israel to freedom, Moses had been reluctant. He was so afraid that he finally said to God, "They're not going to believe me . . . who should I tell them has sent me?" God said to Moses, "You tell them that *I AM WHO I AM* sent you." (See Exod. 3:13–15.) From that time on the phrase or name "I AM" meant only one thing to the Jews—it meant "I AM GOD."

When Jesus said the words "I AM" in the garden that night, the crowd was supernaturally thrown to the ground. Jesus whipped a little deity on them, if you will; He laid a real heavy God-trip on them. It was easy for Him, because He *was* God.

Then they came and gruffly seized Jesus. When those who were standing around saw what was

> about to happen, they said to Him, "Lord, should we strike them with the sword?" Simon Peter drew his sword and struck the high priest's servant, cutting off his right ear. (The servant's name was Malchus.) But Jesus said, "Enough of this!" He touched the man's ear and healed him.
>
> Then He told Peter, "Put your sword back into its sheath. Everyone who uses the sword will die by the sword. Don't you understand that even now I could call to My Father and He would send Me more than twelve legions of angels? But then how would the Scriptures be fulfilled that say it must happen like this? Shall I not drink the cup the Father has given Me?" (Matt. 26:50b–54; Mark 14:46–47; Luke 22:49–51 TGL, p. 239)

It's at this point Jesus' disciples get into the act. One of them says to Jesus, "Lord, shall we strike with the sword?" Before Jesus could even reply, our friend Peter decided to make things happen. Though surrounded by hundreds of enemies, most of them armed soldiers, Peter takes out his long knife and begins to fight. He slashes at the head of Malchus, a servant of the high priest. As Malchus ducks, however, Peter cuts off his ear. (Some say that even if Peter had wanted to say he was sorry, Malchus couldn't have heard him!)

Can't you hear swords coming out of their sheaths as

the Roman soldiers see violence erupting? Jesus, however, calms things down by saying to the crowd, "Permit even this" (Luke 22:51 NKJV); in other words, *It stops here!* This keeps the crowd from pouncing upon Him and the disciples and killing them on the spot. He then takes Malchus's ear and reattaches it to the servant's head. Finally He turns to Peter and says, "Do you think that I cannot appeal to My Father and He will at once put at My disposal more than twelve legions of angels?" (Matt. 26:53 NASB). Twelve legions of angels is seventy-two thousand angels! In other words, *Thanks, Peter, but no thanks! I have everything perfectly under control.*

> At that same time Jesus said to the crowds and to the chief priests, the captains of the temple, and the elders, who had come out to arrest Him, "Have you come out to seize Me with swords and clubs as if I were a robber? I sat daily with you, teaching in the temple, yet you didn't arrest Me or stretch out your hands against Me. But this has all happened to fulfill the Scriptures of the prophets. This is your hour and the power of darkness." (Matt. 26:55–56a; Mark 14:48–49; Luke 22:52–53 TGL, p. 239)

He's implying, *What are you doing here at night, as though I'm going to run, or be secretive? I was with you every day in the temple. Why didn't you arrest Me then?* Christ is not very happy here. It's true He remained calm, dignified, and powerful while being arrested. But He was careful to point out their inconsistencies. He wanted His enemies to know just how hypocritical and wrong they were in arresting Him.

The whole show of force, with several hundred soldiers and police bearing weapons, came across as ridiculous to Jesus. He forcefully rebuked them for their sickening charade. They treated Him as a criminal, and presented themselves as the protectors and enforcers of the law. Yet He'd committed no crime whatsoever. Even if He'd done so, they could have found Him any day in the temple, for He never tried to hide from the authorities.

Jesus continued by saying, "But this has all happened to fulfill the Scriptures of the prophets. This is your hour and the power of darkness" (Matt. 26:56a; Luke 22:53b TGL, p. 239). In essence, *Okay, now we're going to let Satan do his thing; this is your hour . . . Satan is going to work through your rebellious heart.*

Throughout this ordeal Jesus remained in total control. Though everyone around Him was scared and confused, He was in perfect command of the situation. Always calm and considerate of the needs of others, He willingly submitted to His captors though He could have commanded angelic fury against them. His desire to "drink the cup" the Father had given Him was more important than anything else. Thus, He was led away in chains and the disciples fled in fear.

THE TRIALS OF JESUS

We'll now walk with Jesus as He's taken through six separate trials on His way to the Cross. Many people don't realize that on the night before His crucifixion, He was subject to three religious and three civil trials. The religious trials took place before a man named Annas, before the Supreme Court of Israel, then culminated with a religious sentencing at about five o'clock that morning. Then came the civil trials: the first before Pilate, the second before Herod, and the third again before Pilate. Every one of these trials was a sham, a lie, and a rip-off. They made an absolute mockery of law and justice. But Jesus knew this was coming when He said, "This is your hour and the power of darkness."

Friday, 1:30 a.m.–3:00 a.m.
Trial number one—Jesus appears before Annas

We read: "Then the cohort of soldiers and the chief captain and the officers of the Jews took and bound Jesus. They led Him away first to Annas because he was the father-in-law of Caiaphas, who was the high priest that year. (It was Caiaphas who had advised the Jews that it would be prudent for one man to die for the people.)" (John 18:12–14 TGL, p. 240).

Before we go further, let's explore this character named Annas. As you know, the Romans of that day ruled over Israel much like the Russians ruled over Poland (and other countries) after World War II. For many reasons, the Jews were difficult for the Romans to control. Thus, they said to the Jewish people, "Okay, we'll allow your leaders to rule over you—the high priest and his family, and the Supreme Court and the Pharisees and the Sadducees—if they'll all play our game. We are still over you, but we'll allow your leaders to have some local control."

This man, Annas, had been high priest for many years. Finally, the Romans came to him and said, "Annas, we really like you, but it's time for you to step down. Do you have any sons?" Annas said, "Yes, I have a few sons." So the Romans said, "Pick one of your sons to be the ruling high priest." They liked Annas because he played their game.

After a few years they came again to Annas and said, "Do you have another son?" Actually, Annas had five sons, and all of them successively served as high priest. Years later, when the Romans came and asked if there were even more sons, he said "No, but I have a son-in-law named Caiaphas." This man, Caiaphas, was the ruling high priest during the time of Christ. Actually, he was a token high priest—the power behind it all was Annas, something both the Romans and the Jews knew to be true.[1]

Here's something else about Annas and his family—they were rich. Do you know why? They were big-time crooks. For example, when someone went to the temple to sacrifice a lamb, the officials would say,

"Hey, wait a minute. You can't just bring any old lamb in here—you need a 'temple-approved' lamb." And, of course, temple approval came at a cost. Also, Annas and the temple officials ran a money-changing operation within the temple grounds. They would demand a special currency, then sell it at an inflated rate of exchange. It was shameless robbery.

This is why Jesus, not too many days before His arrest, walked into the temple and did some housecleaning. He took out a whip or some kind of woven cord, and drove the animals out of the temple. He then turned over the money changers' tables and said, "My Father's house will not be a den of thieves!" At this, yea, verily, verily, Annas was really ticked off!

It appears Jesus had been getting under Annas's skin for a while. Annas didn't like the fact that Jesus was popular with the people. This made him and the other religious leaders look bad. And now that Jesus had disrupted the money-changing scheme at the temple, Jesus hit Annas right where it hurt most: his wallet.

For these reasons, Annas was thrilled to have Jesus brought his way in the middle of the night. He knew that he needed to move fast, while the people of Jerusalem were still asleep. Every Jew and his brother was there for the Passover. Annas couldn't afford a religious riot on his hands; his goal was to see Jesus convicted of an offense—any offense—that would convince Pilate Jesus was worthy of death. With luck, he could have Jesus crucified before the crowds knew what was happening. But if people woke up to find Jesus in Annas's custody, it wouldn't be a pretty sight. Annas needed things to move quickly.

JEWISH LAW

To better understand what was happening, let's examine some aspects of Jewish law. First, a person was not obligated to incriminate himself, much like our Fifth Amendment today. After a person was charged with a crime, the accusers would present their case, then the defenders, and finally a bunch of lawyers would try to figure out who was lying. Never did the accused have to speak unless he chose to.

In this first trial of the evening, every basic rule of Jewish law was broken: no charges were read, no witnesses were allowed, and no evidence was presented. Instead, Annas began his interrogation of Jesus: "The high priest questioned Jesus about His disciples and His teaching" (John 18:19 TGL, p. 240). In essence, *Jesus, tell us how You have perverted Your followers with Your teaching.* He was trying to get Jesus to admit that He taught for the purpose of a revolution, for the overthrow of the Roman Empire. By doing this, however, Annas was totally out of order, legally speaking. His goal was to get Jesus to speak, and thus incriminate Himself. Annas was way out of bounds.

It makes sense, then, that Jesus would reply the way

He did: "I spoke openly to the world. I always taught in the synagogues and in the temple where all the Jews assemble. I said nothing in secret. Why do you question Me? Question those who have heard Me. They know what I said" (John 18:20–21 TGL, p. 240).

By saying this, Jesus was calling Annas to order. But Jesus' display of calm authority and directness angered one of the temple guards. "When He said this, one of the officers standing nearby struck Jesus in the face. 'Is this the way You answer the high priest?' he demanded. 'If I spoke wrongly,' Jesus answered, 'explain my error. But if I have spoken rightly, why do you strike Me?'" (John 18:22–23 TGL, p. 240). It was illegal to strike a person who was accused but not yet proven guilty.

Well, Annas was not getting very far with Jesus. It was obvious he wasn't going to get self-incriminating information from his prisoner. He did, however, stall long enough to allow the Supreme Court of Israel to gather in the middle of the night in order to hear the case.

Friday, 1:30 a.m.–3:00 a.m.
Trial number two—before the Supreme Court of Israel

The second trial of the evening took place in front of Caiaphas and a group of leaders called the "Sanhedrin," the Supreme Court of Israel. This court, which consisted of seventy men plus the high priest, needed a quorum of at least twenty-five members present to carry on their business.

Hurriedly, they met in Caiaphas's house in the middle of the night to begin this wicked trial of Jesus. It was an illegal act, for it was against the law for them to meet or rule at night. Yet there they were, at two or three o'clock in the morning, breaking their own rules in order to put Jesus on trial.

In order to get the picture, imagine a large room that looks similar to our courtrooms of today. There was a section where the rulers sat together, with the high priest sitting in front of them. The accused was placed directly in front of the authorities. Around the courtroom stood various accusers and defenders—lawyers who were trying to determine the truth—as well as spectators near the back of the room.

On this particular evening the Supreme Court had a problem—they had no legal charge against Jesus. By law they needed two witnesses who would agree on specific charges against Him. Also, they were under pressure to act quickly, for morning was coming soon. What did these distinguished leaders do? They got off their ecclesiastical bottoms and approached the spectators in the audience, seeking two witnesses that would agree on a charge against Jesus. It was a travesty of justice. Sadly, they found a couple of clowns who both agreed they'd heard Jesus make a statement against the temple: "I will destroy this temple made with hands, and in three days I will build another made without hands" (Mark 14:58 NASB).

What was the charge? That He would somehow wreck the temple. The leaders knew this wasn't a charge serious enough to stand before Pilate. They knew it had taken forty years to build the temple, and it would take more than three days to tear it down. Obviously, Jesus had been talking about His body; Caiaphas and the Supreme Court realized the charge wouldn't stick.

With time running out and dawn approaching, Caiaphas made his move. Occasionally, when the court was at a standstill—when it couldn't figure out who was telling the truth and what was going on—something very intense would happen. The high priest would stand and raise his right hand, thereby putting the accused under oath before him and before God. It was as if he were saying, *Okay, clear away the witnesses, clear away the lawyers, clear away anyone who's said anything about anything. I'm now acting for God as His spokesman for all of Israel. I now put you under oath, and am going to talk to you directly!* Under Jewish law, the accused was then obligated to talk.

The Bible tells us Caiaphas stood once more and said, "Are You the Messiah, the Son of the Blessed One? I charge You under oath by the living God: tell us whether You're the Messiah, the Son of God" (Matt. 26:63; Mark 14:61 TGL, p. 242).

You see, the Jews believed in a triune God: the Father, the Son, and the Holy Spirit. The priest wasn't saying, *Are you a god?* No, he was saying, *Are You God the Son. I adjure You!*

There are some people who say this was the greatest moment in Christ's life. Look at His response. Here He is, exhausted. He's already been in the garden and almost died, remember? He knows the answer He's about to give is going to cost Him His life. Yet, "'It's just as you have said,' Jesus answered. 'I AM. Furthermore, I tell all of you that later on you will see the Son of Man sitting by the right hand of power and coming on the clouds of heaven'" (Matt. 26:64; Mark 14:62 TGL, p. 242).

I AM . . . I AM . . . I AM . . . and by the way, boys, the next time you see Me, I'll be coming on the clouds of heaven!

The high priest was not happy when he heard Christ's response. He reached up and tore his priestly garments, which in that day was a sign of great disgust. This is what a person would do if someone raped their daughter and took away her virginity, or if someone did something very grievous to them or their loved ones. By tearing one's clothes, a person was saying, *I'm so disgusted over what I've just heard that I don't ever want to wear these garments again.* "Then the high priest tore his clothes and said, 'He has spoken blasphemy! Why do we need any more witnesses? Listen, you have heard His blasphemy. What do you think?' 'He deserves to die!' they answered. Everyone condemned Him as deserving death" (Matt. 26:65–66; Mark 14:63–64 TGL, p. 242).

Now things became ugly. Some of the leaders spat in Christ's face and struck Him with their fists. Has anyone ever hit you with his fist? Even in boxing, the participants wear thickly padded gloves. If you've seen pro wrestling on television, you know most of that stuff is fake. But a buddy of mine went to a match where two wrestlers really did get mad at each other—he said there was blood all over that ring. I can tell you, these were real punches that were striking Jesus' face. They blindfolded Him and then struck Him, saying, "Since You're a prophet, prophesy who hit You." They may have even pulled His beard out in chunks, for the Old Testament speaks of that happening. They pulverized Him, mocked Him, and called Him filthy names. Those who accused Him of blasphemy were themselves blaspheming against His very name.

Jesus, however, stood and received it all. Do you know why? Because Jesus loves us so much it hurts. He was willing to "drink the cup" the Father had given Him. As we'll soon find out, this was just the beginning of His physical and spiritual suffering on our behalf. Things will get much worse for Him before the trials are over.

6

Peter Tries to Follow Jesus Incognito

Imagine the confusion in Peter's heart after the events in the garden. Jesus had just given Himself over to His enemies, and all the disciples had run away in fear and cowardice. To Peter, it must have felt as if the world were caving in on top of him! He ran hard and fast, hoping to elude capture under the cover of darkness. Eventually, when he realized he wasn't being followed he slowed to a walk, allowing the thoughts in his head to catch up with him. He then buried his face in his hands. Even now the dissonant arguments in his mind drowned out the thumping heart in his chest. This was a crisis of belief—should he continue to run away from the action? Or should he turn back and stand with Christ during this hour of darkness? He knew what he had to do; Peter turned back toward the city.

> Simon Peter and another disciple were following Jesus. Because this disciple was known to the high priest, he went with Jesus into the high priest's courtyard, but Peter had to wait outside at the door. The other disciple, who was known to the high priest, came back, spoke to the girl on duty there and brought Peter in. "You are not one of this man's disciples, are you?" the girl at the door asked Peter. He replied, "I am not." (John 18:15–17 NIV)

FOLLOWING AT A DISTANCE

Peter was at a crossroads. If he remained far from Jesus, he would be safe but not live up to the boasts and promises he'd made earlier. On the other hand, if he stood by Jesus, he would live up to his promises but could easily lose his life. No doubt he was truly tormented as he pondered what to do. Unfortunately, Peter made a huge mistake—he tried to strike a balance between both paths. The Bible says that "Peter followed him at a distance." He chose the way of compromise.

In studying Peter's denials, it's easy to come down on him harshly for his failure. What's often forgotten, however, is the fact that Peter did have a love for, and sense of loyalty to, Christ. Something was drawing Peter to Jesus. If he hadn't loved Jesus, he wouldn't have considered pursuing Him. His love and loyalty, therefore, compelled him to consider turning back. However, Peter's love for Christ was too weak to give him strength to return and stand at Jesus' side. His weak love—and weak faith—were not enough to resist compromise. So, out of his weakness, he decided to follow Jesus from a distance.

There was another reason, though, that Peter wanted to be near Christ. He must have remembered his arrogant boasts about his willingness to die for his Lord. Even though Jesus had told him that those prideful statements were untrue, Peter still felt he had something to prove. Due to destructive pride, he felt compelled to live up to his boasting. No doubt, his own words echoed through his troubled mind. Remember, he had said things like: "Even if all are made to stumble because of You, I will never be made to stumble" (Matt. 26:33 NKJV). "Even if I have to die with You, I will not deny You!" (Matt. 26:35 NASB).

Peter didn't want to completely abandon Christ. But he desperately wanted to prove that Jesus' predictions about Peter's desertion were wrong. His pride would not allow him to act against his ill-advised boasts. So, "Peter followed Him at a distance." Unfortunately, anytime we act to protect our pride a fall is soon to come. Peter learned this lesson the hard way, as we'll soon see. Years later, in one of his letters to the early church, he wrote these words: "God resists the proud, but gives grace to the humble" (1 Pet. 5:5 NKJV).

Besides all this, Peter was incredibly curious to see

what would happen to his Master. Would Jesus stand up against His accusers and call thousands of angels to His defense? Or would He meekly follow the road leading to death? Peter loved to be where the action was; he hated being far from the excitement. He was determined to find out how it all would end. Curiosity got the best of Peter.

Curiosity can often get us into trouble, isn't that true? The problem with Peter's curiosity was that it wasn't mixed with conviction or reverence. He just wanted to know how things would turn out. In some ways, he was like the children of Israel in the Old Testament, who were curious to see what was in the ark of the covenant. The ark was a wooden chest, covered with gold, and made to hold some of the most precious artifacts of Israel's early history. In essence, the ark represented the presence of God to the Israelites, and God clearly warned them to never touch it or peek inside. One day, however, curiosity got the best of some Israelites. They peered inside and paid a dear price.

> God struck down some of the men of Beth Shemesh, putting seventy of them to death because they had looked into the ark of the Lord. The people mourned because of the heavy blow the Lord had dealt them, and the men of Beth Shemesh asked, "Who can stand in the presence of the Lord, this holy God? To whom will the ark go up from here?" (1 Sam. 6:19–20 NIV)

Curiosity can get us into trouble, and that's what happened to Peter.

Perhaps above all else, Peter was afraid. For Peter to stand with Jesus at this point would have taken an incredible amount of courage. Those who arrested Jesus would've known Peter as the one who cut off Malchus's ear. This means Peter was in danger for two reasons: he was a follower of Jesus, and he'd also attempted to murder an important person in religious circles. This wasn't a good scenario, and Peter knew it.

The truth is, Peter was under no spiritual compulsion to be near Jesus that dreadful night. Christ had already announced to His disciples they would flee. If Peter wanted to be with Christ, he should have gone back to stand with his Master and not hide under cover of darkness. He made the grave mistake of trying to have it both ways. Yes, he followed Christ, but at a distance.

Friend, it's always dangerous to follow Jesus from a distance. There is no one more conflicted and paralyzed than a Christian who tries to follow Jesus halfway. In fact, Jesus says He would rather have His followers hot or cold, rather than lukewarm: "I know your deeds, that you are neither cold nor hot; I wish that you were cold or hot. So because you are lukewarm, and neither hot nor cold, I will spit you out of My mouth" (Rev. 3:15–16 NASB).

The Bible is full of warnings—given to God's people—of the perils of trying to follow both God and the flesh. It never works, as Peter soon found out.

SETTING THE SCENE

So Peter turned back and soon found himself outside the courtyard of the high priest's residence. John, the beloved disciple, was already inside the courtyard due to the fact that his family must have been known to Annas. Maybe John's family, as prominent fishermen, provided fish for those working and living in Annas's household. Whatever the case, John was well known by many in the courtyard that evening.

One commentator says this about John and Peter:

> Perhaps John saw Peter through the gate; he stepped outside, spoke a few words to the door maid, secured her permission, and thus enabled Peter to enter, doing his friend an ill-service. The reason why John recounts all these details is because he is taking full blame. Instead of reminding Peter of the warning of Jesus and taking Peter away, John—even John himself—helps to make Peter disregard the warning.[1]

Apparently John left Peter in the courtyard and went into the hall where Jesus was being tried. This left Peter alone with the enemies of Jesus who were gathered around a small fire. Remembering and deeply regretting his attack on Malchus, Peter must have felt what little courage he had slipping away. He was cold, so he approached the charcoal fire warily, careful to disguise himself in the darkness. There's no way he wanted to be recognized.

LESSONS TO LEARN

Peter did just the opposite of what Christ wanted him to do. He should have been off alone with God in prayer, seeking answers and understanding. Or perhaps spending time with the other disciples, seeking together what God was teaching them in this darkest of hours. Instead—sadly—Peter walked into a trap. He found himself in an environment so full of danger there was no hope of leaving unscathed. How presumptuous of Peter to throw himself into temptation. He was truly blind to his weakness, unaware of the plans of the enemy. He had ignored the wisdom found in the proverbs of Solomon: "A wise man is cautious and avoids danger; a fool plunges ahead with great confidence" (Prov. 14:16 TLB).

Peter didn't join Christ's enemies in order to defend the truth; rather, he was trying to hide in their midst. Thus, the stage was set for Peter to commit the tragic sin of denying his Lord. He had

- revealed his pride and overconfidence,
- demonstrated his inability, or unwillingness, to understand himself,
- demonstrated his prayerlessness,

- revealed his independent attitude,
- demonstrated his impulsiveness,
- followed Jesus from a distance,
- presumptuously walked into temptation,
- and sat with the enemies of Christ.

It's easy to shake one's head and be disgusted at Peter's attitude and actions. But let's remind ourselves of what the apostle Paul wrote in his first letter to the Corinthians:

> All these things happened to them as examples—as object lessons to us—to warn us against doing the same things; they were written down so that we could read about them and learn from them in these last days as the world nears its end. So be careful. If you are thinking, "Oh, I would never behave like that"—let this be a warning to you. For you too may fall into sin. (1 Cor. 10:11–12 TLB)

THE DENIALS BEGIN

So here is Peter, sitting around a charcoal fire in the middle of Annas's courtyard, hiding himself among those who'd arrested Jesus. Filled with a mixture of fear and uncertainty, he desperately wanted to avoid recognition as one of Jesus' followers. For a short time his identity remained unknown. Then, out of the corner of his eye, he noticed a young servant girl staring at him intently. She was the girl who'd opened the gate and let him into the courtyard. Little did he know he would soon do the unthinkable—he would deny the Master he'd sworn to serve.

The young girl had left her post at the gate and made her way to the fire around which Peter was seated. She wanted to see if Peter was who she thought he was—a follower of Jesus. She knew that John was a follower of Christ—maybe this man was too. Also, she must have wanted to make herself look important in the eyes of those around the fire. One author commented: "She wanted these men to know she knew something they did not know. They were talking about Jesus and what had just taken place, and yet did not know right in their own midst there sat one of Jesus' own disciples. All, no doubt, caught their ears when she made her assertion."[2]

She blurted out to Peter, "You are not one of His disciples, are you?" For some reason she didn't mention the name of Christ. Maybe she didn't know Jesus' name, or perhaps she considered it beneath her in some way. Peter answered resolutely: "I am not." Peter failed Jesus by denying any association with Him or His disciples.

How could this happen? Peter was a large man, strong and willful. How did this little girl become such a threat to a bold fisherman? Certainly, the question came from a source he never would have expected. Peter must have been eyeing the soldiers around the fire, examining their slightest move, looking for any hint they recognized him. He must have calculated just how quickly he could draw his sword if challenged; how far he was from the gate in order to escape; how many soldiers he'd need to kill in order to survive. But a servant girl? He never saw it coming, and her question sliced him deeper than any sword could.

Suddenly exposed, Peter quickly moved to limit the damage. Impulsively and without forethought, he fell back to who he'd been apart from Christ. Caught off guard by Satan's cunning, he lied to the girl by denying his Lord. One commentator described it this way:

> As many have observed, the girl and what she said were relatively harmless and did not deserve such a drastic response. Peter, however, realized that many ears were listening. Peter's response is called a denial. The word "deny" is used in the New Testament as the polar opposite of the word "confess." We are to confess (i.e., acknowledge) Christ but deny ourselves (i.e., disown our private interests for the sake of Christ). Peter here does the reverse. He denies Christ in order to save his own interests.[3]

A SECOND SERVANT GIRL

We read: "One of the high priest's servants, a relative of the man whose ear Peter had cut off, challenged him,

'Didn't I see you with him in the olive grove?' Again Peter denied it, and at that moment a rooster began to crow" (John 18:26–27 NIV). Matthew 26:71 describes the high priest's servant as "another girl" (NIV).

His identity revealed, Peter could no longer sit near the fire. He got up and stood near the edge of the courtyard, probably close to the gate in case he needed a quick escape. Nervous and somewhat embarrassed, he worked to remain inconspicuous. He didn't need more attention coming his way—he moved slowly so as not to arouse more suspicion.

Near the gate was a small porch from where he could make his escape, if needed. But Peter had already yielded to sin by denying Christ the first time, and now more temptation was drawing near. In spite of his subtle precautions, it wasn't long before another servant girl pointed him out to the crowd. This girl didn't ask a question, however—she spoke with certainty and conviction. "This fellow was with Jesus of Nazareth," she exclaimed (Matt. 26:71 NIV). The Bible says she was a "relative of the man whose ear Peter had cut off" (John 18:26 NIV). She might have been in the garden when Jesus was arrested, we don't know. But she knew this was the man who'd tried to kill her relative, and she could speak as an eyewitness of his true identity.

Peter's heart pounded in his chest. The soldiers' stares were now cold and threatening; his worst fears were coming true. In imminent danger of arrest and death, Peter lashed out in self-defense. Again he denied any involvement with Christ, this time with an oath: "I don't know the man!" (Matt. 26:72 NIV). To strengthen his case, and to make his deceit sound more convincing, Peter used an oath. In essence, he said, *As God is my witness, I say to you I don't know the man.* For a Jew to take an oath before God was a serious act. In fact, Peter forgot Christ's command regarding oaths: "I tell you, Do not swear at all: either by heaven, for it is God's throne; or by the earth, for it is his footstool; or by Jerusalem, for it is the city of the Great King . . . Simply let your 'Yes' be 'Yes,' and your 'No,' 'No'; anything beyond this comes from the evil one" (Matt. 5:34–37 NIV).

It's said that anytime a Jew took an oath, even when not using God's name explicitly, the person was calling God as witness to the truth of their statement. By this act, Peter was insulting God, for as the Bible says, "It is impossible for God to lie" (Heb. 6:18 NIV).

Amazingly, he attempted to pull God into the middle of his shameful deceit. Even more, Peter belittled Christ by saying, "I don't know the man!" One commentator said, "Oh how dreadful for him to call Christ 'the man,' when he had boldly declared that he was the Son of God! What a terrible fall was this!"[4] It seems impossible for Peter to deny Jesus more severely than he already had. Yet Satan was not finished with his temptations; Peter's heartbreaking fall was not complete.

THE THIRD DENIAL

The account continues:

> About an hour later another asserted, "Certainly this fellow was with him, for he is a Galilean." Peter replied, "Man, I don't know what you're talking about." Just as he was speaking, the rooster crowed. The Lord turned and looked straight at Peter. Then Peter remembered the word the Lord had spoken to him: "Before the rooster crows today, you will disown me three times." And he went outside and wept bitterly. (Luke 22:59–62 NIV)

Why Peter didn't leave the courtyard after his second denial, we'll never know. Luke writes in his Gospel that Peter stayed in this place of temptation for another hour. What kept him there? Perhaps it was his real, yet weakened love for Jesus; perhaps his curiosity demanded he see the turn of events. Most likely, Satan himself tempted Peter to linger in the palace courtyard when he should have fled. Whatever the reason, Peter remained where he shouldn't have been, for reasons he shouldn't have had.

As time passed, the enemies of Jesus must have been emboldened as they heard of Jesus' sufferings before Annas. Peter, out of nervousness and fear, began to converse with those around him. This is what sealed his doom, for people in Jerusalem could easily recognize the accent of a Galilean, which they despised. It's been said that "the Galileans spoke with a burr; so ugly was their accent that no Galilean was allowed to pronounce the benediction at a synagogue service."[5] It was his mouth that got Peter into trouble.

Those in the courtyard were now convinced that Peter was a disciple of Christ, for they knew that Jesus and His disciples were from Galilee. Peter's accent was the last piece of evidence needed to prove his association with the accused. They said to Peter, "Surely you are one of them, for your accent gives you away" (Matt. 26:73 NIV). The truth was out, and now Peter felt trapped, afraid and desperate. Instead of admitting his identity, however, he upped the intensity of his denials. "He began to call down curses on himself, and he swore to them, 'I don't know this man you're talking about'" (Mark 14:71 NIV).

John MacArthur wrote an interesting note about this, Peter's third denial: "'To curse' is a very strong term that involved pronouncing death upon oneself at the hand of God if one were lying. In perhaps the most serious taking of the Lord's name in vain that is conceivable, Peter said, in essence, 'May God kill and damn me if I am not speaking the truth.'"[6]

By now, Peter had made a fool of himself and broken God's heart in the process. There he stood, raging out of control, calling down curses upon himself one after the other. The louder he became, the more he was saying to those around him, *I am alone. I am afraid. I am a liar.* How pathetic the situation had become. Just a few yards away, Jesus was being beaten for Peter, while Peter was cursing and denying the very Christ who loved him. What a tragic moment during Christ's walk to the Cross.

Yet when all appeared hopeless God stepped in to save Peter from himself. In the middle of Peter's third and most vehement denial a rooster crowed, calling forward the dawn and calling Peter to repentance. What a small, ordinary thing—a rooster. Yet God often uses the small and ordinary to fulfill His plans. After all, wasn't it a little servant girl who began the questioning of Peter? God's perfect timing was at play, causing this small animal to close the curtain on Peter's denials.

No one knows how far Peter would have fallen if not interrupted. There are those who say Peter could have denied Christ even to the degree Judas had. We'll never know. When Peter heard the rooster's shrill cry he immediately remembered Jesus' words, "Before the rooster crows today, you will disown me three times" (Luke 22:61 NIV). It was a miracle with a message, and Peter heard it loud and clear. What was God saying to Peter through the rooster's crowing? I believe He was assuring Peter He was still in control, and that He had not abandoned him in spite of his betrayal. Certainly, Peter was reminded that Jesus knew all things, for His prophecy of the event had been spot-on. Perhaps too, God was assuring Peter that it was a new day—the time for repentance had come.

THE GAZE OF JESUS

At this same moment, Peter looked up and saw Jesus standing in front of him, looking intently into his eyes. The Bible tells us, "The Lord turned and looked straight at Peter" (Luke 22:61 NIV). Caught up in his denials, Peter hadn't noticed what was taking place around him. He didn't see Jesus being led his way. One author stated, "The temple police were just then leading [Jesus] from the hall of trial through the open courtyard to some place of detention until he should be wanted again. With His face contused, black and blue from the blows He had received, with spittle still defiling His countenance, Jesus looked upon poor Peter."[7]

Can you imagine what crashed through Peter's mind as he caught the gaze of Jesus? He must have been shocked, embarrassed, and full of shame. He knew that Jesus had heard his denials—the look on Jesus' face made that clear. Yet I believe no one in all of history has received a look like the one Jesus gave to Peter. In the original language we get the idea that Jesus gave Peter "a look, or gaze, of clear discernment."[8]

Jesus did not seek to shame or expose His friend. Nor did he rebuke Peter, or look away in disgust. Rather, He gave Peter a look that only Peter would understand. Jesus' gaze held many messages for His friend: *You have broken My heart and hurt Me more than My enemies ever could; I must rebuke you for you are lying; I heard all your denials; but I have not forgotten you—I still love you!*

In other words, Jesus would not repay Peter in kind. Though Peter had vehemently denied Jesus, Jesus would never deny Peter. Nor did He ignore Peter, which would have been the way of a lesser man. Instead, Jesus took the time and emotional effort to cast a look of love toward Peter. It was this love that melted Peter's heart and led him to repentance.

BITTERNESS AND REPENTANCE

Then we are told: "And he went outside and wept bitterly" (Luke 22:62 NIV). To his credit, Peter responded with godly sorrow. He turned and left the courtyard immediately. Where did he go? Perhaps back to Gethsemane to pray, or most likely he stumbled who-knows-where, his vision blurred by darkness and tears. Wherever it was, he couldn't escape the pain and anguish that now flooded his soul. Earlier in the garden he'd found it difficult to pray; now prayer gushed out of him in heaving sobs. At last, in utter brokenness and humble dependence, he could do nothing but pray. His strength was gone. His pride was leveled. Yet he was not alone, for God was with this broken, weeping man.

What a sight this must have been. Strong, powerful Peter, now a man with his face in the dirt—broken before

God. The Bible tells us that he "wept bitterly." One translation says, "He went out and cried and cried and cried" (THE MESSAGE). Finally, he was aware of his sin—alone before God—reliving each detail of his dreadful actions. As he sat alone in the darkness, he may have felt beyond the reach of God's comfort. Yet Peter was expressing godly sorrow, which leads to a right relationship with God. We're told in 2 Corinthians 7:10, "Godly sorrow brings repentance that leads to salvation and leaves no regret, but worldly sorrow brings death" (NIV).

LESSONS TO LEARN

Being sorry for our sin is never enough. Only repentance, which means a change of mind or a change of course, can heal the heart of man. Worldly sorrow brings remorse, guilt, and depression; godly sorrow is caused by the conviction of the Holy Spirit. Worldly sorrow embitters a man; godly sorrow brings desire to change. Worldly sorrow leads to death; godly sorrow leads to a repentant heart.

Peter, alone in the darkness, wept tears of godly sorrow. But with those tears came repentance, something that would radically change Peter for the years to come. He must have wondered if he'd ever again enjoy Christ's love and acceptance. For now, that kind of comfort seemed far away.

What Peter didn't know was this: within a few hours

he would encounter the risen Christ, who would assure him of His love and a future role in His kingdom plan. In this all believers find hope and comfort as we face our own personal failures. What grace and mercy Jesus has shown to Peter, and to us.

7

Jesus Confronts Hard Hearts

Friday, 3:00 a.m.–5:00 a.m.
Trial number three

We now come to trial number three, where the sentencing of Jesus took place. By law there was to be a buffer of twenty-four hours between the conviction and the sentencing of an individual. In Jesus' case it was only two. After His appearance before Annas, it appears the leaders put Christ into a holding area, possibly placing Him in a dungeon nearby. We don't know if He had food or water, but He sat there for at least two hours. Then they brought Him out for sentencing.

> As soon as daylight came, all the elders of the people—both the chief priests and the teachers of the law—met together against Jesus to execute Him. They brought Him up to the whole Sanhedrin and said, "If You are the Messiah, tell us."

> He said to them, "If I were to tell you, you would certainly not believe. And if I were to ask the questions, you would not answer Me or let Me go. But from now on the Son of Man will be seated by the right hand of the power of God!"
>
> "So You are the Son of God?" they all said.
>
> "It's just as you say," He replied, "because I AM."
>
> "Why do we need further witnesses?" they said. "We have heard it ourselves from His own mouth!" Then the whole crowd arose and tied up Jesus and took Him to appear before Pontius Pilate, the governor. (Matt. 27:1–2; Mark 15:1; Luke 22:66–71; 23:1 TGL, p. 244)

Here it is, five o'clock in the morning, and Jesus is brought back to court for sentencing. They said to Him, "Now let's go through this one more time. Are You the Messiah?" Christ responds with an answer that, at first, seems a bit confusing. He says, "If I should tell you, you wouldn't believe." Of course, He was right. Though these leaders of Israel were familiar with Psalm 22, Isaiah 53, and other Old Testament prophecies that spoke of the Messiah, they didn't recognize that God's Anointed stood before them. Instead, they were looking for a Messiah who would destroy the Roman Empire, then immediately rule for a thousand years. They weren't buying this "die-for-the-sins-of-the-people" bit.

In essence, Christ was saying, *Even if I tell you what*

the Messiah is really like, you won't believe Me. Then He continued: "If I should ask you a question you won't answer Me." This was not Jesus' first encounter with these guys—throughout His ministry He'd talked with them many times about this very subject. He knew their hearts were hardened.

Then the leaders said to Jesus, "So You are the Son of God?" If they could catch Jesus blaspheming God's name, they would be just in putting Him to death—blasphemy was a capital offense under the law. Of course, Jesus wasn't blaspheming, and both His life and words proved that fact. The leaders, however, chose to ignore His teaching, His miracles, His power, and the fact that He fulfilled the Old Testament messianic prophecies. They were blinded to the truth of His claims. Thus, they relegated Him to the status of a simple mocker and blasphemer. When Jesus answered truthfully by saying, "It's just as you say: 'I AM,'" the leaders found what they were seeking. They stood up and cried, "He deserves to die," then grabbed Him and bound Him and took Him to the Roman governor, Pontius Pilate.

JUDAS'S TRAGIC END

During Jesus' trial in the courtroom, a different drama was unfolding outside the city gates. Do you remember Judas "how-can-you-do-this" Iscariot? He'd had his moment in the sun, and now he was failing.

> When Judas, who had betrayed Him, saw that Jesus was condemned, he was overcome with remorse. He returned the thirty pieces of silver to the chief priests and the elders and said to them, "I have sinned by betraying the blood of an innocent man!" "What does that matter to us?" they replied. "Deal with that yourself." Judas threw down the pieces of silver in the temple, left, and went out and hung himself. (Matt. 27:3–5 TGL, p. 244)

Evidently Judas had been following the trials of Jesus to see the outcome of his treacherous betrayal. When he saw that Jesus was going to be put to death, he had a change of mind. This guilt-ridden man realized he was partially responsible for the innocent Christ being tortured and sentenced to die.

Before realizing the consequences of his sin, Judas enjoyed being the center of attention. He delighted in his newfound power and the money that had come his way. But now, with guilt deep in his heart, the awfulness of what he'd done lay heavy on his soul. The thirty pieces of silver he'd wanted so badly now haunted him, leaving him empty. He hurried to the chief priests, seeking to remove his guilt by giving back the money.

Judas was mistaken, however, if he thought he'd receive consolation from the chief priests and elders. They had used him for their own wicked plans. Now they wanted nothing to do with Judas, and they were irritated that he would bother them at such an important hour. Instead of helping bear his guilt, they cruelly sent him away, saying, "What does that matter to us? Deal with that yourself." If only Judas had been truly repentant. If only he had asked forgiveness for his horrible sin. Instead, he was overcome with guilt and despondency. Throwing the silver at the feet of the elders, Judas fled the temple, found a tree overhanging a cliff, and hanged himself. What a tragic end for Judas Iscariot.

Friday, 6:00 a.m.–7:00 a.m.
Trial number four

JESUS BEFORE PILATE

We now come to one of the greatest confrontations in the Bible—that between Jesus Christ and a Roman governor named Pontius Pilate. The Jewish leaders hated Pilate, and they despised the fact they had to seek his permission to put Jesus to death. Yes, they had passed their own judgments, but the Romans had the last word in matters of capital punishment. Even worse, it was now Passover weekend, a time of heightened political and social tension. The leaders knew Pilate would be cautious during this major Jewish holiday.

To be sure, Pilate hated the Jews as much as they

hated him. Why? Pilate was feeling pressure from his boss, Tiberius, the Roman caesar of that day. Tiberius was a cruel and paranoid individual, known to kill people for the slightest offense—or none at all.[1] This meant that Pilate and other provincial governors were subject to the whims of a crazy man. Tiberius would often enjoy making his governors look foolish, and he had the power of life and death over each of them. The fact that Pilate was ruler over Jerusalem means he must have been low on the totem pole, for Jerusalem was hated by the Romans. Believe me, Pilate hated the Jews—he absolutely despised them.

A Jewish historian tells us that Roman soldiers would wear full dress gear with a picture of Tiberius on the side of their breastplates. The Romans worshiped Caesar as god, so anytime a Roman wearing this emblem walked by a Jew, the Jew was expected to raise his hand and say, "Caesar is lord." Do you think the Jews were buying into that act? I don't think so.

Other historians tell of how Pilate would often taunt the Jews. One time he marched his soldiers into Jerusalem, in full uniform, to see if the people would recognize Caesar as lord. The Jews, of course, refused. Pilate threatened them, saying, "Either you say that Caesar is lord or I'll cut off your heads." Defiantly, the Jews went down on their knees and stretched out their necks before the soldiers, saying, "Go ahead and cut off our heads—we will never say Caesar is lord. No, Jehovah is Lord!"

Again, just before a Sabbath when the Jews were lighting candles and beginning their chants, he sent his soldiers to the streets to mock and make fun of them. At other times Pilate would order Jews killed for no reason. The Romans hated the Jews, and the Jews hated the Romans. And Pilate hated these Jewish leaders, and they hated him back.[2]

So here they are, in Pilate's courtyard, early this Friday morning. On one side were the Jewish leaders—on the other side, Pilate. Between them was the greatest Jew who ever lived—Jesus the Messiah. We're talking high drama here.

> Then the Jews led Jesus from Caiaphas to the Roman judgment hall, where Jesus stood before the governor. Because it was early, they did not go into the judgment hall. (They didn't want to become defiled and be unable to eat the Passover.) So Pilate went out to them. "Of what are you accusing this Man?" he asked them.
>
> "If He were not a criminal," they answered, "we wouldn't have brought Him to you." "Take Him and judge Him according to your law," Pilate replied. "We aren't permitted to execute anyone," the Jews responded. (In this way they were fulfilling what Jesus said about the kind of death He would suffer.) (Matt. 27:11a; John 18:28–32 TGL, p. 245)

SETTING THE SCENE

Pilate didn't stay in Jerusalem very often—it was too slow for his tastes. He lived up north, in Caesarea, which was the San Francisco of that day. When in Jerusalem, however, he lived in a huge fort in the middle of the city, called the Praetorium. He would live there during seasons that were volatile, such as during Passover. During these times he would move his entire proceedings to Jerusalem—his wife, the kids, and everyone else with him. It was from this fort that Pilate would rule the people. During hot weather he would rule inside, but in the cool of the morning he often went out to a giant walkway that angled down to the ground. This is where he stood, talking to the Jewish leaders.

The Jews, with all their man-made rules, refused to enter Pilate's palace. During the Passover they were forbidden to touch anything that was "gentile"; if they did so they'd get religious "cooties." This would disqualify that person from eating the Passover meal, which was the highlight of their celebration.

You see, right from the start they're pushing Pilate. Can you imagine—it's early in the morning and he's getting out of bed, shaving, when a servant comes to him and says, "Hey, Pilate, we have several thousand Jews outside in the courtyard." Pilate says, "Well, what do they want?"

"Well, they're pretty upset with the man named Jesus."

"Okay, have them come in, as many as can, and I'll deal with this case."

"But they don't want to come in."

Why not? Spiritual "cooties"! Can't you see Pilate rolling his eyes? In any case, Pilate goes outside to meet them.

PILATE'S FIRST QUESTIONS

At first, everything goes smoothly. Pilate says to the leaders, "What accusation do you bring against this man? What's the charge?" Are you ready for this? They don't have a charge. They didn't want to say to Pilate, "See this pathetic, bleeding Jew right here? He says He's God! And that makes us mad." If they'd started with that, Pilate would've replied, "Take your hocus-pocus religion and get lost!"

No, they didn't have a formal charge so they had to ad-lib. They said, "Look, Governor . . . we are the Supreme Court of Israel. Do you think we're here on Passover weekend because we want to be here? Don't you think this is a little bit serious? Pilate, just give us the go-ahead to kill Him." Pilate, however, was in no mood to play their game. Besides, this was a great opportunity for him to stick it to the Jews, whom he despised. So he said to the leaders, "You have your own law—do what you have to do." This forced the leaders to say through their teeth, "We are not permitted to put anyone to death."

They must have hated this, having to admit they were subject to Roman law. They didn't realize, though, that by seeking a Roman death penalty, they were actually helping to fulfill prophecy. Here's what the Gospel of John has to say: "'And I, if I am lifted up from the earth, will draw all men to Myself.' But He was saying this to indicate the kind of death by which He was to die" (12:32–33 NASB).

Did you know that if the Jews had killed Christ instead of the Romans, Christ would not have been crucified for your sins? He would have been stoned to death. Apparently, God didn't want Christ to die by way of stoning. Why not?

It may be that stoning would have resulted in Christ's dying too quickly. A number of years ago I read about a man who was stoned to death in Iran. People buried him up to his waist, and then threw rocks the size of grapefruits at him. He was dead within fifteen minutes. Don't get me wrong—that's not a fun way to die. But it doesn't come close to what took place on the cross. Stoning is gruesome, but not near as gruesome and humbling as was the Crucifixion. Evidently God wanted His Son, Jesus Christ, to die a horrible death and to be lifted up for all to see. Maybe He knew by the time we modern Americans arrived we'd need something graphic to get our attention. The Crucifixion does get our attention, and rightfully so.

FALSE ACCUSATIONS

> They began accusing Him, saying, "We found this man subverting our nation and forbidding us to give tribute to Caesar. He says He's the Messiah, a king." The chief priests and elders continued making many accusations against Jesus. But He made no reply. "Do You refuse to answer?" Pilate said. "Don't you hear how many accusations they're charging You with?" Jesus remained silent, not answering a single charge. The governor was astonished. (Matt. 27:12–14; Mark 15:3–5; Luke 23:2 TGL, pp. 245–46)

The first two of these charges—being a bad influence and not paying taxes—weren't going to work with Pilate, for all Jews were trying to renege on paying taxes to Caesar. The third accusation, however, got Pilate's attention: ". . . saying that He Himself is Messiah, a king."

Can't you see what Pilate was thinking? *A king? There is only one king—Caesar. What will happen if Tiberius hears that on Passover weekend, of all weekends, there was a man walking around and telling the crowds, "Hey, I am a king."* After all, this was the one weekend each year when Jews celebrated their freedom from the Egyptians. Pilate didn't want them talking about freedom from Rome. For sure, this third item got Pilate's attention.

As for Jesus' reaction to the charges, yea, verily, verily—Jesus blew Pilate's mind! Pilate was used to people groveling before him, pleading for mercy. After all, he had the power to sentence them to crucifixion, one of the cruelest ways to die ever known to humankind. Pilate had seen people cry, lie, plead, curse, spit . . . you name it, he'd seen it. Yet here was Christ, standing before him in total dignity—silent before the charges pouring in against Him. Was He beaten and bleeding? Yes. Was His hair matted from sweat and blood mixed together? Yes. But amazingly, He denies Pilate's demand that He defend Himself. Standing calmly, Jesus doesn't utter a word.

As crude as Pilate was, he was also smart. He decided to take Jesus inside where the Jews wouldn't follow. He wanted to talk with Jesus one-on-one, hearing firsthand what this was all about.

> Pilate then went back to the judgment hall and called Jesus. "Are you the King of the Jews?" he asked Him. Jesus replied, "It's just as you say. Are you asking this on your own, or did others tell you about Me?" "Am I a Jew?" Pilate answered. "Your own nation and the chief priests handed You over to me. What have You done?" Jesus said, "My kingdom is not of this world. If My kingdom were of this world, My servants would fight to keep Me from being handed over to the Jews. But at present My kingdom is not from here." (Matt. 27:11b; Mark 15:2; Luke 23:3; John 18:33–36 TGL, p. 246)

Pilate must have thought to himself, *You've got to be kidding me! Is this some kind of joke?* He wasn't mocking Jesus as much as he was mocking the Jews who'd brought Jesus before him. *Is this the best they can do?* So he approaches Jesus as if to say, *Come on . . . You obviously aren't a king, and they obviously aren't dealing with a full deck, right? You're not really a king, come on.*

When Pilate asked if Jesus was the King of the Jews, the reply was straightforward. *Yes, you're right . . . it is as you are saying. But do you really care, Pilate, or are you just wanting to know?* This made Pilate mad, and he responded, "Am I a Jew?" In essence he was saying, *Am I a dog?* He hated the Jews. "Am I a Jew? Your own nation and the chief priests delivered You up to me. What have You done?" *You must have done something really awful to be in so much trouble. The Jewish leaders, on Passover weekend, deliver You—a Jew—to a Gentile whom they despise. Buddy, You must be in big trouble!*

To hear Pilate speak these words must have broken Jesus' heart. The Bible says Jesus came to His own, yet His own people received Him not. They rejected Him and threw Him to a Gentile. These statements must have cut Jesus to the core, but He remained cool and calm in the midst of Pilate's insults.

Jesus replied, "My kingdom is not of this world. If it were, my servants would fight to prevent my arrest by the Jews. But now my kingdom is from another place" (John 18:36 NIV). He says, *Look, Pilate, I am no threat to the Roman Empire. For one thing, I don't have an army. If I did, don't you think they'd be fighting for Me right now? Don't you think they would've begun fighting the moment I was arrested? I have no army, for My kingdom is not of this world.* Jesus does have a kingdom, and someday He will reign for a thousand years from Jerusalem, during the millennial kingdom. Jesus' kingdom has no boundaries, but for now it is not of this world.

Of course, all of this goes over Pilate's head: "'Then You really are a king?' Pilate said. Jesus answered, 'It's just as you say. I am a king—I was born for this, and for this I came into the world, so I might testify to the truth. Everyone who belongs to the truth hears My voice.' 'What is truth?' Pilate asked" (John 18:37–38a TGL, p. 246).

You know what Jesus is saying? He's claiming to be the king of reality! Here's a simple definition that describes truth: truth is reality the way God sees it. If you say, "Dawson, I want to know the truth about life, about the reality of eternal life." Then go to the King of truth, Jesus Christ. If you really want to know the truth, you can find it in Jesus Christ.

By this time Pilate is in no mood to discuss truth. He spins and heads back to the crowd, yelling back over his shoulder, "Hey, buddy, what is truth?" What is truth! Jesus had basically said, *I am the way, the life, and the truth,* and that terrible morning Pilate never caught the clue. This proud Roman had no doubt heard philosophers talk about truth and had come to the conclusion that searching for truth was useless. Tragically, he turned away from the only person who would have shown him ultimate truth.

The Jews had accused Jesus Christ of being a threat to the Roman Empire. Pilate, after interviewing Jesus, was convinced He was no threat at all. In fact, he considered the charges brought against Jesus to be absurd. After all, how could this pitiful peasant Jew—beaten, worn down, near collapse—be a threat to the mighty Roman machine? He was no threat. Pilate knew it, Jesus knew it—and the Jews knew it. So Pilate went outside to tell the Jews exactly what he thought. Basically, he wanted to tell them to take a long walk off a short pier: "After saying this, Pilate went out again to the Jews and said to the chief priests and the crowds, 'I find this Man guilty of nothing.' But they strongly insisted, 'He is stirring up the people. He is teaching throughout Judea, starting from Galilee and reaching even to this place'" (Luke 23:4–5; John 18:38b TGL, p. 246).

When Pilate heard them mention Galilee his ears perked up. Why? Pilate didn't rule over Galilee, a guy named Herod did. And guess who happened to be in town that weekend? You guessed it—Herod. So Pilate did what any self-seeking pagan ruler would do—he decided to lateral this political time bomb over to Herod. With friends like Pilate, you wouldn't need enemies.

Friday, 6:00 a.m.–7:00 a.m.
Trial number five

JESUS BEFORE HEROD

> When Pilate heard this, he asked whether the Man was a Galilean. On learning that He was from the jurisdiction of Herod, he sent Him up to Herod, who happened to be in Jerusalem at the time. When Herod saw Jesus, he was quite pleased. For a long time he had wanted to see Him since he had heard many reports about Him and hoped to see Him perform some miracle. He probed Him with many questions. But Jesus didn't answer them even though the priests and teachers of the law stood there viciously accusing Him.
>
> After Herod and his soldiers had ridiculed and mocked Him, they clothed Him in a gaudy robe and sent Him back to Pilate. From that day on Pilate and Herod became friends; before this they did not get along. (Luke 23:6–12 TGL, pp. 246–47)

It appears God brought all the boys in the band to Jerusalem for this great moment in history. Let me tell you about Herod. Herod was a godless man, so much so that he'd stolen his brother's wife and made her Mrs. Herod. That's fairly serious, when you rip off your brother's wife. Herod was the one who arrested John the Baptist and put him in jail, in a dungeon. Herod was a spooky, religious guy, and sometimes he'd bring John out of prison in order to talk with him. One day he did this, and there sat Mrs. Herod on the throne next to her husband. The prophet looked straight into Herod's eyes and said, "It is not lawful for you to have your brother's wife." This made Mrs. Herod very upset.

From here you may know the rest of the story. Mrs. Herod had a daughter from her previous marriage, and evidently she was a thing of beauty. One evening Herod threw a huge party at the palace, and this young lady got up and danced for the king. It must have been something very exotic, for Herod, drunk with both lust and wine, said to the girl, "I will give you up to half my kingdom." All this over a dance? The girl met with her mother for a few moments, then returned to the king and said, "I don't want half the kingdom—I want John the Baptist's head." When Jesus heard that Herod had beheaded John, with a broken heart He went away to pray. He loved John the Baptist. In fact, He once said, "In all humanity there is no one greater than John" (Luke 7:28 TLB).

Jesus was fully aware that Herod was an evil man; Herod's ways sickened Him. Both superstitious and godless, he was the man Jesus had once called "that fox" (Luke 13:32 NIV). Herod, though, was excited to meet Jesus, hoping to see some miracles. He wanted to see magic tricks, like some cheap entertainment at the circus. Herod thought to himself, *Jesus is in a predicament here; maybe He'll put on a performance if it means He can go free.* But Jesus didn't comply. Herod continued to press for entertainment by asking questions: "Where are You from? . . . Did You really do such and such a miracle? . . . Did You really raise Lazarus from the dead?" On and on it went, but Jesus stood calmly without saying a word.

After a while this became awkward. Herod realized he didn't want to get mixed up with this political hot potato, so he mocked Jesus by having his soldiers pretend to worship Him. Herod got a few cheap laughs, then sent Jesus back to Pilate.

You say, "Dawson, can we learn anything from this encounter between Herod and Jesus?" Yes, at least one thing. It's serious business when Jesus won't talk to you. At some point, God will quit talking to every person who rejects Him. We never know when that moment will come.

8

Pilate Panics

Friday, 7:00 a.m.–8:30 a.m.
Trial number six

We now come to Jesus' sixth and final trial. No one knows how Pilate felt when he saw the Jewish leaders and the soldiers bringing Christ back from meeting with Herod. We can safely assume he wasn't happy, for he'd been hoping that Herod would take care of the situation. Now, however, he was caught in a difficult dilemma. He knew Jesus was innocent of the charges against Him, but he also knew the Jews would complain to Caesar if he didn't act. On top of this, people were now waking up and making their way to the courtyard. Perhaps two or three thousand spectators were now crowded into the palace grounds, curious to see Jesus on trial. Pilate needed to make this "Jesus problem" go away—in a hurry.

> Then Pilate called together the chief priests and the rulers of the people and said to them, "You

brought this Man to me on the charge of stirring up subversion. Yet on examining Him I found no substance to your accusations. Neither did Herod because he sent Him back to us. You can see He's done nothing deserving death.

"Now, you have a custom directing me to release one man to you at Passover. So I'll punish Him and then release Him." (At the feast the governor's custom was to release one prisoner to the people, whomever they chose. At that time a notable prisoner named Barabbas was being held along with a few of his fellow insurgents. He was a robber who had been thrown into prison for an insurrection in the city and for murder.)

When the crowds had gathered and noisily asked Pilate to act on the custom, he answered, "Whom do you want me to release to you? Barabbas, or Jesus, who is called 'Messiah'?" (He knew the chief priests had handed Jesus over because of envy.) (Matt. 27:15–18; Mark 15:6–10; Luke 23:13–19; John 18:39–40 TGL, p. 247)

THE BARABBAS TRICK

Passover was an especially volatile time in the city of Jerusalem. Every year, Jews from all over Israel would gather to praise God for His ancient deliverance from Pharaoh and the Egyptians. In my mind's eye I can imagine some of them saying, *Oh, isn't God wonderful and isn't God great.* Then someone else might say, *Yes, and God is incredibly powerful.* Then I imagine another person saying, *Yeah, and God could do it again . . . today!* Pilate was thinking fast . . . he knew if he wasn't careful, a riot could break out, and quick.

So Pilate devised a plan. He remembered that each year the Romans would release a Jewish prisoner during Passover—a gesture of goodwill. He decided to use this to his advantage: he would give the people a choice between Jesus and a hardened criminal named Barabbas (which means "son of a rabbi," or "preacher's kid"). This Barabbas guy was bad news—he was a robber, a murderer, and pretty much a slime bucket. Pilate thought to himself, *Surely if I hold up Jesus on one side and this terrible guy on the other, the crowd will choose to release Jesus. There's no way they will choose Barabbas over Jesus!*

I find it interesting that Pilate, acting out of expediency, decided to change his leadership style on the spot. He goes from totalitarianism (one man rules), to democracy (many people rule). He said to the Jewish leaders, "Maybe we should have a vote about Jesus," knowing that Jesus was very popular with the common people who now crowded the courtyard.

At that very moment, however, Pilate's plan was ruined by his dear wife, Mrs. Pilate. It appears she'd been awakened earlier that morning when Jesus was first brought to the palace. As Jesus was sent to Herod, however, she fell back to sleep and suffered a horrible nightmare. We don't know exactly what she dreamed, but the bottom line was this: *Please don't mess with Jesus, for He is a righteous man. I've suffered many things on account of this dream.* Just as Pilate was to present the vote to the crowd, an aide tapped him on the shoulder and said his wife needed to see him. In the few minutes he spent talking with his wife, the religious leaders worked the crowd. They saw what Pilate was planning, and they worked the masses in a hurry.

> The chief priests and the elders stirred up the crowds to ask Pilate to release Barabbas to them instead, and to execute Jesus. "Which of the two do you want me to release to you?" the governor said. "Do you want me to release to you the King of the Jews?" They replied, "Barabbas!" They all shouted together, "Not this Man! Get rid of Him, and give us Barabbas!" (Matt. 27:20–21; Mark 15:9–11; Luke 23:18; John 18:39–40 TGL, p. 248)

These Jewish leaders must have said to the people, "Hey, do you want to show Pilate how much we hate him? Do you want to make a statement to the Roman Empire? Look, Pilate has become a Jesus-lover, and he wants Him released. Do you want to stick it to Pilate and the Roman Empire? Vote Barabbas!"

These leaders worked the crowd so fast that, by the

time Pilate turned and took the vote, it was too late. You may be thinking, Dawson, that's crazy. How can a crowd turn like that in such little time? If you've been to the Middle East, you know how volatile crowds can become. Maybe you've seen clips on television from Iran and other countries—perhaps funeral marches or massive protests. If so, you can picture what the crowd in Pilate's courtyard must have looked like.

At this point Pilate realizes he's losing this out-of-control shouting match. The Barabbas trick didn't work, so he now tries plan B: the "sympathy-of-the-crowd" trick. This trick was simple: he would take Jesus back inside, beat Him nearly to death, then show Him to the people. Hopefully they would feel sorry for Jesus, tell themselves enough is enough, and allow Jesus to go free. *Maybe that will work,* thought Pilate.

THE SCOURGING OF JESUS

"Pilate took Jesus and had Him flogged" (John 19:1 TGL, p. 248). The Bible is gracious about this act of scourging; so matter of fact. Yet we know from historical sources what a cruel practice this was in the Roman arsenal. Soldiers would tear all the clothes off a victim then tie his hands to a pole, leaving him hunched over with his back exposed. The scourge itself, called a "cat of nine tails," was a sturdy stick with nine strips of leather attached to it. At the end of each strip was a hard leather ball, and along the sides were woven pieces of sharpened bone and iron. According to Roman law, a trained soldier was to swing the scourge into the victim's back, while another trained soldier would watch his breathing to make sure he didn't die. Scourging was called the half-death—it wasn't intended to kill a person, but rather leave him just short of death.

As you can imagine, the jagged pieces of bone and metal would dig into the victim's body, pulling out chunks of flesh. With only a few strokes the flesh could be torn clear to the muscle, even to the bone. Thus, they pummeled Jesus until He was barely alive. Remember, this is the second time within a few hours Jesus has nearly died: first in the Garden of Gethsemane, and now under the flogging of Pilate's soldiers. Only this time He's turned into holy hamburger—a human wreckage.

"Pilate then came out again and said to them, 'Look, I am bringing Him out to you so you'll know I find Him not guilty.' Jesus came out, wearing the crown of thorns and the purple garment. 'Look at the Man!' Pilate said to them" (John 19:4–5 TGL, p. 248). Pilate was saying, "Look at this pathetic, bleeding Jew. Isn't this enough already? Enough!" Of course, Pilate had no idea his statement of "behold the Man" would become a rallying cry for Christians across the centuries. Believers ever since have said, *Yes, Pilate, we have beheld the Man . . . beaten beyond recognition . . . no longer recognizable as a human being. We have beheld Him, and we love Him!*

When the crowd saw Jesus, however, they were not satisfied. They wanted more blood. Pilate's plan had backfired. The crowd began to chant even louder, "Crucify . . . crucify!" The angry voices must have sounded like thunder rumbling over the courtyard. The bloodthirsty crowd was out of control, on the verge of starting a riot. It's at this point that Pilate had enough! In his anger he yelled at the leaders and said, "You take Him and crucify Him yourself . . . I find Him not guilty" (Matt. 27:23b; John 19:6 TGL, p. 248). In other words, *I dare you to take Him and kill Him. If you do, I'll kick your tail, but I dare you!*

The Jews, however, could see the tide turning in their favor. They responded, "We have a law . . . and by our law He ought to die because He claimed to be the Son of God" (John 19:7 TGL, p. 249). *Listen, Pilate, you want us to respect your laws? Then you respect our laws. You want the bottom-line truth? This Man said He was God. Now that's not going to fly with us . . . He said He was God!*

Oh, Pilate . . . he didn't want to mess with Jesus; he marveled at this Man, and he was trying his best to get rid of Him. He'd encountered Jesus' claim to be a king, but this latest charge—that He claimed to be God—took things to a different level. "When Pilate heard this claim, he grew even more afraid. He returned to the judgment hall and said to Jesus, 'Where do You come from?'" (John 19:8–9 TGL, p. 249).

Pilate was inquiring, *What planet are You from again? Where did You say You were born? From where . . . to whom . . . for what . . . ?* But Jesus wouldn't answer. Do you know why? He'd already told Pilate His kingdom was not of this world. This made Pilate even more frustrated.

"'You refuse to talk to me?' Pilate said. 'Don't You know I have authority to crucify You—or to release You?' Jesus answered, 'You would have no authority at all over Me unless it had been given to you from above. Because of this the one who handed Me over to you is guilty of the greater sin'" (John 19:10–11 TGL, p. 249).

Jesus is so gracious, even under great stress. He was saying, *Hey, Pilate, you think you're in control, but God's allowing this to happen. You're a bit player on a big stage. You didn't deliver Me up, the Jews did. And they're the ones who have the greater sin.* Jesus' recognition of Pilate's authority, His reference to God's power, and His graciousness to Pilate strengthened the governor's belief that Jesus was absolutely innocent.

> Pilate said to them, "Should I crucify your king?" "We have no king," the chief priests answered, "except Caesar!" When Pilate saw he couldn't dissuade them, but instead a riot was in the making, he took water and washed his hands in front of the crowd and said, "I am innocent of the blood of this righteous Man. You will be witnesses of the fact." All the people answered, "His blood be on us and on our children!" (Matt. 27:24–25; John 19:15b TGL, p. 249)

One last time Pilate goes out to the crowd. This time, however, the Jewish leaders reveal their final ploy—it was like a dagger thrust deep into Pilate's heart. They sneered, *Oh, we get it—you're a Jesus lover. Well, we're going to tell Tiberius Caesar of this Jesus who said He was a king, and how you sided with Him. Wait until he hears this news!* The leaders had succeeded—now Pilate was completely panicked!

Let's be clear here—God loves His people, the Jews. They are His chosen people, and through the Jews came His Son, Jesus Christ. God is pro-Jewish. But I want to tell you something . . . the Jewish nation has been paying for this ever since. Can you think of a nation anywhere in the world today that is more hated than the Jewish nation? Can you think of a people more scattered, more humiliated, more killed than the Jews? And as we near the last days, we know they'll continue to be despised until the very end. Jesus Himself will come back and save the Jews from total annihilation.

But look at Pilate. He didn't want to be in the position he was in. He knew there was something unique about Jesus, and he tried to get rid of Him as best he could. Still, Jesus kept coming and coming until finally Pilate was forced to make a decision. His life or Christ? His job or Christ? His future or Christ? That's always what it comes down to, isn't it? It's not Christ *and* something, but rather Christ *or* something. God forces each of us to make a decision regarding Christ. Unfortunately, Pilate chose his way instead of Christ. He decided to turn against Jesus and have Him murdered. Barabbas was released, but Jesus was handed over to be crucified.

> Their voices and those of the chief priests won out. So Pilate, wanting to satisfy the crowd, ordered that they should get what they demanded. He released Barabbas to them—the man they had asked for, who had been thrown into prison for insurrection and murder—but he gave in to their demands about Jesus and handed Him over to be crucified. (Matt. 27:26; Mark 15:15; Luke 23:23b–25; John 19:16 TGL, pp. 249–50)

Pilate's role in the drama is now over. No one really knows what happened to him after that fateful day. Some ancient traditions say he committed suicide by falling on his own sword; others say Tiberius Caesar finally kicked him out of power and exiled him to an island for the rest of his days. This much we do know, however—after these events we don't ever hear about Pilate again. He was a bit player on a huge stage, and he made the wrong decision.

THE HOUR HAD COME

Friday, 9:00 a.m.–12:00 p.m.

Jesus Christ was born to die, and now the hour had come. The darkest moment in all of human history was at hand.

The cruel and illegal trials of Jesus Christ had come to a close. Exhausted and beaten, Jesus was about to face the most torture-filled death in human history. But before He was nailed to the cross, He had to endure even more mockery and a painful walk from the Praetorium to the place of crucifixion, which was called "the Skull."

> Then the governor's soldiers took Jesus and led Him away to the court called the Praetorium. There they gathered the whole company of soldiers around Him. They stripped Him, then again clothed Him in purple, and put a crimson cloak on Him. And they put on His head the crown of thorns they had made, and placed a reed in His right hand. They continued mocking Him, bowing in homage and saying, "Hail, 'King' of the Jews!" They spat on Him and took the reed from Him and kept beating Him on His head.
>
> When they finished ridiculing Him, the soldiers stripped Him of the cloak and the purple garments and gave Him His own clothing. Then they led Him out to crucify Him. (Matt. 27:27–31; Mark 15:16–20 TGL, p. 250)

This battalion, like all others, consisted of four to six hundred men, some of whom wove thorns the size of sewing needles into a crown, forcing it onto Jesus' head. They then took a reed, or stick, and used it to smash the crown even farther into His skull. If you want to experience pain, try sticking needles into your head. We've all banged our head against a cabinet or a door or something sharp. Imagine—these soldiers pounded this crown into Jesus' skull!

The soldiers then stripped Jesus of His clothes and put a purple robe and a red cape on Him. Evidently, they had Him sit in a chair, put the reed or stick in His hand, then approached Him one by one to bow in mock worship. They then spat in His face and grabbed the stick and hit Him with it. Finally, they draped His clothes back over His bleeding body and led Him to be crucified.

PAINFUL STEPS TO CALVARY

We now come to Jesus' final steps to the Cross. Some scholars say it was roughly eight hundred yards from Pilate's palace to Golgotha, or "the Place of the Skull." That's the equivalent of eight football fields in length, all at a steady uphill incline. Nearly dead from the beatings He'd received, Jesus now begins His death shuffle through Jerusalem's narrow streets: "Jesus went out, carrying His own cross. As they were going, they found a passerby from Cyrene coming in from the country. He was named Simon, the father of Alexander and Rufus. They grabbed him, laid the cross on him, and forced him to carry it behind Jesus" (Matt. 27:32; Mark 15:21; Luke 23:26; John 19:17a TGL, p. 250).

In that day criminals were made to carry their own cross to the place of crucifixion. This was one more humiliation put on the guilty person. Remember, during His ministry Jesus had told His disciples, "If any man will come after me, let him deny himself, and take up his cross, and follow me" (Matt. 16:24 KJV). He was very clear about what He was saying . . . a person who follows Christ must be willing to die for Him.

We don't know if Christ carried the whole cross, or just the cross beam. Whichever it was, His back was so shredded by the scourging that He must have experienced intense pain. The Bible tells us He stumbled and fell to the ground, unable to carry it farther. Seeing this, a Roman soldier thought it would be funny to make one Jew carry the cross for another. A man was randomly picked out of the crowd; his name was Simon the Cyrene. It's curious, isn't it, that this man's name—and his sons' names—are recorded in the Bible. In God's perfect irony, Simon's sons—Rufus and Alexander—may have became leaders of the early church[1] (see Rom. 16:13). It's very possible this event led Simon and his boys to become followers of Jesus, leading them to help turn the world upside down for the gospel. God always gets the last laugh.

"A large crowd followed Him, including women who were weeping and mourning for Him" (Luke 23:27 TGL, p. 250). In the Middle East, from that day even until now, people often wail and shriek and weep uncontrollably during times of great crisis. They are able to show much more emotion than we do in the West. That's the picture we have here as Jesus continues His march to the Cross. Many women were weeping and mourning for Jesus, and they weren't necessarily of His disciples. Maybe they'd heard Him speak, or were somehow aware of His ministry. Perhaps they'd never seen a person as beat up as Jesus was. Whatever the reason, these women were wailing and screaming at the pitiful sight of Jesus stumbling to His death.

In response, Jesus stops for a moment and turns to them, saying,

> Daughters of Jerusalem, don't weep for Me but for yourselves and for your children. The days are coming when they will say, "Blessed are the childless, and the womb that never bore children, and the breasts that never nursed!" Then they will begin to say to the mountains, "Fall on us!" and to the hills, "Cover us!" For if they do these things when the tree is green, what will happen when it is dry? (Luke 23:28–31 TGL, pp. 250–51)

Jesus was predicting that horrible things would befall the Jews because of their rebellion against God. God's judgment against Israel would be so severe that childless women would be glad they were childless, having less sorrow to bear. Jesus predicted that people would be in such agony they would cry for the mountains to fall on them.

Sure enough, nearly forty years later (in AD 73), there was a major riot in Jerusalem. By that time Tiberius had long since died, and Titus was Caesar. The Romans responded with what became the worst persecution in Jewish history. The streets of Jerusalem were lined with crucified Jews, and the temple was basically turned to dust. As always, Jesus' words were true—He had predicted these terrible times even as He shuffled His way to the Cross.

As an aside, when you see people turn their backs to Christ today, whom should you pity? Not God, of course, for He's fine without any of us, thank you. No, the Bible says to pity those who are mocking God. We're told it's a "terrifying thing to fall into the hands of the living God" (Heb. 10:31 NASB). That's the essence of what Jesus was saying to these daughters of Jerusalem: *don't weep for Me; rather, weep for yourselves.*

THE CRUCIFIXION

"When they brought Him to the place called the Skull (or in the Jewish language, 'Golgotha' ['Calvary' in Latin]), they offered Him wine mixed with myrrh, but when He tasted it, He wouldn't drink. There, at nine o'clock, they crucified Him" (Matt. 27:33–34; Mark 15:22–25; Luke 23:33; John 19:17b TGL, p. 251).

Finally, Christ arrived at the place of crucifixion. The

Hebrews called this place Golgotha; we call it Calvary. It was referred to as "the Place of the Skull." Why? Some say the mountain resembled the shape of a skull. Others, that the place was littered with skulls from those who'd been killed by the Romans. We don't know for sure. We do know that if Christ hadn't died by late that afternoon, when He did die, rather than being buried, His body would've been thrown in the city dump. Wild animals would have scattered His remains. God didn't allow this, however, for Scripture declared, "Nor did His flesh suffer decay" (Acts 2:31 NASB).

When the crowd arrived at Calvary, the soldiers offered the victims a drink of vinegar mixed with myrrh. This was a knockout drink . . . something to take the edge off the pain. Christ tasted it and spit it out. Why? He'd come to suffer all the pain for our rebellion. He wasn't willing to dull His suffering even the slightest bit. Such is His love for us.

If you've heard anything about crucifixion, you know it's not a pretty death. They took Christ and laid Him on two wooden posts that formed a "T," then drove large metal spikes through His wrists into the cross beam. We often see pictures of Christ with holes in His palms, but the Greek word for *"hand"* can also mean *"wrist."* The palm would have torn from the weight of His body, thus most scholars believe the spikes were driven between two small bones on the inner side of His lower arm. The soldiers were careful to not hit an artery, or He would have bled to death very quickly. Crucifixion was not about dying quickly—most victims suffered seventy-two hours or more before they perished.

After nailing His hands they placed a small block of wood under His back, pushed His knees toward His chest, and then drove a single spike through both feet. The soldiers were careful to keep Jesus' knees high toward the chest; this would allow Him to push up against the block, prolonging His life and, thus, the pain. The Romans had perfected the "art" of using this torture tool. They knew if a victim's arms and legs were outstretched, in a swan-dive position, blood would begin to settle toward the bottom of the body. This would cause low blood pressure and a high pulse rate, allowing the victim to pass out. For this reason, they provided a small wooden block, or saddle, for the victim to sit on. This kept the blood circulating, and the victim would stay conscious in order to experience more pain.

Often a victim's pectoral muscles would freeze, or atrophy, and we can only imagine the level of discomfort that settled in the upper arms, neck, and shoulders. This meant air would come into the lungs, but not escape, causing a person to choke to death. To avoid this the victim would often stand up, placing pressure on his feet in order to relieve pain in the arms and chest. Also, some believe the small saddle was sharply pointed; as the victim struggled and moved in order to find comfort, there was damage to the tailbone as well.

Once Jesus' hands and feet were nailed in place, the

four soldiers lifted up the cross with Jesus on it and shoved it into a hole dug for the occasion. The jolt of the cross falling into the hole must have been a tremendous shock to Jesus' body. This may be conjecture, but I wonder if this is when Christ's bones popped out of joint. I don't know how anyone could stand up on a cross with a dislocated ankle, or knee, or elbow. Yet the Bible tells us when Jesus hung on the cross all His bones were out of joint: "I am poured out like water, and all my bones are out of joint. My heart has turned to wax; it has melted away within me" (Ps. 22:14 NIV).

After even a few minutes on the cross Jesus' body ached violently. The nerves in His hands and feet had been shattered, and He began to experience swelling around the joints and wounds. Infection would have quickly invaded His wounds. Isaiah 53 describes the physical suffering Jesus endured on the cross:

> Surely he took up our infirmities
> and carried our sorrows,
> yet we considered him stricken by God,
> smitten by him, and afflicted.
> But he was pierced for our transgressions,
> he was crushed for our iniquities;
> the punishment that brought us peace was
> upon him,
> and by his wounds we are healed.
> (vv. 4–5 NIV)

HIS WORDS OF FORGIVENESS

It's at this point we hear Jesus' first words from the cross. Though He never wasted words, His utterances from the cross are especially important for us to hear. But remember, in order to speak He had to push against the spike running through His feet, expand His chest to get air in His lungs, and then push the air out while forming words. Each sentence took an incredible amount of effort.

The first statement Jesus made seems off-the-wall—He said, "Father, forgive them, for they do not know what they are doing" (Luke 23:34 NIV). The verb in the Greek is active, meaning Jesus kept on saying this phrase. Perhaps He would rest for a while, then push up and say it again. *Father, forgive them for they know not what they do.* But what exactly is Jesus asking? Were these Jewish leaders worthy of forgiveness? Didn't they know what they were doing? Apparently, due to the hardness of their hearts and their spiritual blindness, they didn't truly understand they were crucifying the Messiah. They thought they were doing God a favor by getting rid of one who blasphemed. In effect, Jesus is saying, *Father, forgive them, for they do not know how serious this crime really is.* They actually thought they were doing God a favor.

Did the Jewish leaders truly receive blanket forgiveness that day? We know there's only one way to be forgiven for our sins, and that's by turning to Christ. The word forgive in this context means "to hold off, or let be."[2] Imagine what the angels in heaven were thinking at this point. They've watched as Jesus was mistreated, brutalized, beaten to a pulp, and now suffocating to death on a cross. This is Jesus, the One before whom they would cover their eyes due to the splendor of His beauty. Don't you think they wanted to instantly and completely destroy the world? Yet now they hear Jesus, the One through whom the world was created, saying, *Father, give them another chance . . . hold off, for they don't know how serious their crime really is.*

Sure enough, several weeks later at Peter's sermon on the Day of Pentecost, many of these same people were convicted of their actions. They stood up and said, "*What shall we do?*" Peter told them to repent and believe in the resurrected Christ, and many of them did. Amazingly, some of your closest friends in heaven may be some of these individuals who crucified Christ. How can this be? It's only because God is absolutely gracious!

His prayer of compassionate forgiveness seems impossible to grasp because it contains so much beauty and love. No doubt, those witnessing the Crucifixion were taken aback by Christ's prayer. Most victims would spit and curse at the crowd, but Jesus prayed for those who were torturing Him.

DEPICTED AS A CRIMINAL

"Along with Him they crucified the criminals, two robbers, one on either side and Jesus in the middle. [And the Scripture was fulfilled which says, 'And He was numbered with transgressors.']." (Matt. 27:35a, 38; Mark 15:27–28; Luke 23:33; John 19:18 TGL, p. 251).

Evidently Pilate hoped to insult the Jews by commanding that two criminals be crucified with Jesus. He must have been thinking, *Okay, since the Jews made me do this, I'll throw up two other Jews as well. Since I have to do one, let's knock off a couple of others too. I'll show them.* But the Jewish leaders used this to further humiliate Jesus; they made sure to put Him in the middle. This allowed the crowds to get very close to Jesus, perhaps within six or seven feet. The leaders wanted them to survey the scene and say, *Look, there's three sickos, but the one in the middle must be the worst of them all.* Again, God has the last laugh, for this was all in fulfillment of Scripture that says He "was numbered with the transgressors" (Isa. 53:12 NASB). Why is this important? It means no matter how low you are, Christ got lower in order to save you. *He was numbered with the transgressors.*

> Pilate also wrote an inscription which they placed on the cross above His head. The accusation said,
>
> THIS IS
> JESUS OF NAZARETH
> THE KING OF THE JEWS.
>
> Many Jews read this inscription (it was written in the Jewish language, in Latin, and in Greek), since the place where Jesus was crucified was

> near the city. So the chief priests of the Jews said to Pilate, "Don't write, 'The King of the Jews,' but rather, 'He said, "I am King of the Jews."'" Pilate answered, "What I have written, I have written." (Matt. 27:37; Mark 15:26; Luke 23:38; John 19:19–21 TGL, p. 251)

As a warning to those who passed by, the Romans would write each criminal's crime on a sign, then nail it to the top of his cross. Notice, though, that Pilate did not post a crime above Jesus; rather, he gave Him a title: THIS IS JESUS OF NAZARETH THE KING OF THE JEWS. He commanded that it be written in the three known languages of the day—Hebrew, Greek, and Latin. This made the Jewish leaders very upset. They went to Pilate and said, *Hey, Pilate, take that down. He's not being crucified because He is the King of the Jews, but rather because He said He is the King of the Jews.* But Pilate was in no mood to negotiate; he did this in order to humiliate the Jews. Again, God gets the last laugh. What Pilate wrote was truth for the whole world to see. This truly was Jesus of Nazareth, the rightful King of the Jews.

CHRIST'S POVERTY ON THE CROSS

> When the soldiers had crucified Jesus, they took His clothes and divided them into four equal parts,

> and rolled dice to see who would get each part. They left out the undergarment, however, which was of one piece, woven from the top down. "Let's not tear it," they said, "but roll for it, to see who will get it." So the Scripture was fulfilled that says, "They divided my garments among themselves, and for My clothing they rolled the dice." (Matt. 27:35b; Mark 15:24; Luke 23:34b; John 19:23–24 TGL, pp. 251–52)

This tells us there were four soldiers guarding Jesus, and they took His last earthly possessions while He hung on the cross. One soldier got His sandals, another His belt, one more got the head gear, and the last soldier took His robe. But then a small problem arose. It seems a follower of Jesus had made him a beautiful seamless undergarment, known as a tunic. It was very beautiful, so the soldiers said, *Let's not tear this up—let's gamble for it.* They did so, thus fulfilling the Old Testament Scripture that says, "They divide my garments among them and cast lots for my clothing" (Ps. 22:18 NIV).

What does all this mean? Personally, I see this as one of the most touching moments of the entire event. How rich is Christ? Very rich! Jesus Christ is the richest person who's ever lived. The Bible says all things were made *by* Him and *for* Him. How poor did Jesus become? So poor that when He hung on the cross, even His clothes were taken from Him. In fact, most scholars believe He was stripped completely naked while hanging on the cross.

In 2 Corinthians 8:9 we're told this: "You know the grace of our Lord Jesus Christ, that though He was rich, yet for your sake He became poor, so that you through His poverty might become rich" (NASB). If you're a believer in Jesus Christ, you are very, very rich. He became bankrupt for us, that we might share in His eternal wealth.

THE "LOGIC" OF MOCKING

> This, therefore, is what the soldiers did. Then they sat down to keep guard over Him. Meanwhile the people stood watching. Those who passed by kept jeering Him, wagging their heads and saying, "Aha! You who would 'destroy the temple and build it in three days,' save Yourself! If You're the Son of God, come down from the cross!" (Matt. 27:36–40; Mark 15:29–30; John 19:24 TGL, p. 252)

Jesus Christ was hardly a picture of strength as He hung on the cross. He was so weak He could barely push Himself up to breathe. But this pathetic sight did not arouse the pity of those who were passing by. The crowds stopped and, with contempt, wagged their heads and screamed insults at Jesus.

Their reasoning was simple. If He was truly the Son of

God as He'd claimed, then He ought to come off the cross. Since that wasn't happening, they concluded He was a fake. He had publicly said He would tear down the temple in three days then raise it back up. *Surely,* they thought, *if He's the Son of God, He ought to have enough strength, right now, to come off the cross.* The fact that He didn't, in their minds, made Him a liar.

> In the same way the chief priests, the teachers of the law, and the elders mocked Him. "He 'saved' others," they said, "yet He can't save Himself." "Let Him save Himself, if He's the Christ, the chosen One of God!" "If He's the King of Israel, let the Messiah come down now from the cross so we may see and believe!" "He trusted in God; let God deliver Him now if He wants Him—since He said, 'I'm the Son of God.'" (Matt. 27:41–43; Mark 15:31–32a; Luke 23:35b TGL, p. 252)

The logic of the Jewish leaders was similar to that of the common man, only with more sophistication. They huddled together in small groups and talked loud enough for Jesus to overhear. They said, *Look, all He has to do is come off the cross and we'll believe in Him . . . that's all He has to do.* Of course, there's a theological term to describe their words: baloney! If Jesus Christ had come off the cross and sat in their laps, they still wouldn't have believed in Him. Their hearts were hardened—they'd already seen Him perform miracles, yet their hearts were cold as stone. One would think these religious leaders would control themselves at the sight of men suffering deep pain. But this wasn't the case. These vile leaders forgot their dignity and let their passionate hatred run rampant: "The soldiers also kept mocking Him. They came to Him offering sour wine and said to Him, 'If You're the King of the Jews, save Yourself' " (Luke 23:36–37 TGL, p. 252).

Jesus was dying of thirst, having lost a tremendous amount of fluids due to His beatings and current state. His tongue was so dry it swelled and stuck to the roof of His mouth. And what did the soldiers do? They took some of their own cheap, Kool-Aid wine and held it close to Jesus' lips. They mocked Him by saying, *If You are the King of the Jews, save Yourself.* They were implying, *Come off the cross, Jesus, and we'll give You something to drink!*

HE WOULDN'T COME DOWN

What an amazing, chaotic scene! The crowds passing by were yelling, *Come off the cross, come off the cross. You're a fake!* The religious leaders were telling Him if He came off the cross they would believe in Him, *blah, blah, blah . . .* The soldiers and even the two thieves were getting into the act. From all sides Jesus was hearing: *Come off the cross! Come off the cross! Come off the cross!* Yet Jesus wouldn't come off the cross. Why? Why didn't He come down and clean house, proving to everyone—then and there—that He was the God of the universe?

There are at least two reasons Jesus stayed on that cross. First, it wasn't His weakness that kept Him there but His strength. No peanut-sized little man was going to tell God what to do. After all, three days later Jesus showed His strength by "kicking the stuffing" out of death . . . it was called "resurrection." Our God is in heaven, and He does what He pleases. He was strong enough to stay on that cross, for your sake and mine.

Second, if He'd not stayed on the cross, you and I would be headed for hell. It was during the last three hours of His crucifixion the Father poured His wrath on the beloved Son. I believe Jesus looked through His puffy, swollen eyes and saw you and me and all of humankind. He must have said to Himself, N*o way, I will not come down. I love each person, and I will hang here as long as it takes to set them free, and pay for their rebellion against a holy God.*

If you don't yet know Him, wouldn't you like to follow a Christ like that? What have you got to lose? He loves you, and He proved it by dying in your place and mine on that horrible, torturous cross.

9

Last-Minute Repentance

Jesus wasn't crucified alone on that lonely hill called Golgotha; there were two criminals led with Him to be put to death. In Luke 23:32–33 we read: "Two others, who were criminals, were led away to be put to death with him. And when they came to the place that is called The Skull, there they crucified him, and the criminals, one on his right and one on his left" (ESV).

I find it amazing how good things often come out of bad. A person's best opportunities are sometimes derived from difficult situations. Perhaps you remember that Britain's Queen Mum died a few years ago. Her name was Elizabeth and her husband was the king of England. She lived to be 101 years old, and when she died the British tabloids filled page after page with stories from her life. One of the fondest memories came out of the dark years of World War II when Hitler bombed London, including the royal castle. The Queen Mum was strongly encouraged by her supporters to leave the city, as many others did, but she refused to go. Each morning, as Londoners appeared from underground subways and hiding places to examine the damage, the queen would walk among them and give them courage. She could have run, but she didn't—she stayed with her people. Thus, the nation's darkest hour became her finest. What's the point? Satan, working through evil men, tried to destroy Christ—yet the cross became a place of triumph over sin, and redemption for humankind. Only God can make that happen.

MORE THAN THIEVES

So who were these two men, crucified at Jesus' side? Most of us have heard they were thieves, but that's incomplete. They were more than petty thieves who would break into people's homes and steal possessions. These were bad boys—murderers. They were bandits who would rob people openly, and sometimes kill them in the process. Most scholars believe they were followers of Barabbas, the criminal whom Pilate released in place of Jesus. Barabbas was a true terrorist, and these guys were probably part of his gang.

So there was Jesus, placed between two notorious murderers. Think how this might look in our day. What if Jesus were put to death alongside Charles Manson and Jeffrey Dahmer, two infamous criminals of our own time? Or Richard Speck, who killed a number of nurses near Chicago in the 1960s? Or even Ted Bundy, who may have killed more than fifty women? Again, picture Jesus with Timothy McVeigh on one side and Osama bin Laden on the other. Are you with me? There was Jesus in the middle.

Evil men placed Jesus in the middle of criminals to discredit Him. God allowed this, however, in order to prove His Son is at the center of all things. When a prophet named Isaiah predicted the Messiah would be "numbered with the transgressors" (Isa. 53:12 NIV), he said He would be considered as bad, if not worse, than the men surrounding Him. Pilate didn't know the Old Testament, and the Jewish leaders had no interest in fulfilling prophecy. Yet God was working behind the scenes in order to fulfill His Word.

Why did God allow His Son to be defamed in this way? Why did Christ have to be crucified in the middle? I believe God has a message for a lost world. He's saying, *No matter how lost you are, no matter what you've done or failed to do, Jesus Christ has come down to be among you.* He came for sinners, He lived for sinners, and He died and rose again for sinners. When the Bible uses the word transgressor, it means someone who chooses "to break away from authority."[1] It describes a person who steps over the line without caring what God thinks. It's impossible to find a more powerful word for *sinner* in the Old Testament. What's God saying by having Christ crucified in the middle? He's saying, *I love you, I care about you. I'll go as low as I have to go in order to bring you to Myself. And you can never sink so low as to be beyond My love.*

Friend, I want you to understand this message of Christ being in the middle. Perhaps you feel covered with shame because of the way you've lived. Maybe there's a permanent scar across your self-esteem because of what you've done, or what someone's done to you. Without the power of Christ, that scar will never go away. Jesus was draped between two criminals as a visual aid, to help you understand you're never beyond His love. He can rid you of shame—He can give you a new life.

THE POWER OF SHAME

Shame is a powerful thing. I frequently receive calls on my radio program from abused people who are filled with shame. I tell all of them: "You have enormous value before a mighty God."

Why can I tell them that? I can say this because two thousand years ago Jesus hung on a cross between two criminals. If you ever want to lead someone to Christ, just tell them about Jesus on the cross with a thief on either side. Even if they can't read, they'll understand that message! With this one powerful snapshot, Jesus exclaims, *I love you, I love you, I love you . . . and I can prove it, because I was numbered with the transgressors.*

Jesus will be at the center of all things, for all time. The Bible calls Him a mediator. He's a middleman—the only one—between us and God. You could also say He's our lawyer, representing us before the Father. When Satan accuses you, telling you you're no good, please remember two things. First, God considers you of tremendous value; and second, we have a lawyer, Jesus Christ, who pleads our case before the Father. Jesus was there with these two guys on the cross, and He'll be there with you too.

THE YES OR NO DECISION

Having looked at the significance of Jesus' dying with criminals, let's now examine the thieves' reaction to Christ. In doing so, we'll see a stark contrast between the two roads that lead to eternity. One thief said yes to Jesus; the other said no. Both were forced to make a decision. Many people want to stay undecided when it comes to Jesus, but God doesn't give us that option.

"The robbers who had been crucified with Him started to reproach Him in the same manner. One of the criminals continued to bitterly scorn Him. 'Aren't You the Messiah?' he said. 'Then save Yourself and us!'" (Matt. 27:44; Mark 15:32b; Luke 23:39 TGL, p. 252).

So here are two thieves, with a glimmer of hope in their eyes. Do you know why? The religious leaders were saying to Jesus, *Hey, Messiah, come off the cross if You can—save Yourself.* The thief knew it was a long shot, but it was the only hope he had. So he joined in: *Go ahead, save Yourself and us!* Surely they'd heard that Jesus could perform miracles. Maybe He'd perform one now and save them in the process. Of course, Jesus didn't save Himself or them, crushing their hopes and leaving them furious. The Bible says both of them began to insult Jesus, adding their voices to those of the Jewish leaders and the crowds passing by. I find this shocking. By now you'd think they'd have bonded with Jesus, all being in the same predicament. They shared the same sentence, the same physical suffering, were all stripped naked and experiencing shame together before the crowds. Why didn't they bond? Perhaps they sensed Jesus was different. They somehow knew He could act if He wanted to—yet He chose not to. For this reason they became angry.

Have you ever been angry with God? It's easy to be amazed at the hardened hearts of these two criminals, but the Bible tells us we all suffer from the same human condition: rebellion against God. None of us understands all that God understands; in fact, we are born into misunderstanding. If He had not revealed Himself to us, we would be forever darkened in our knowledge of Him. Is that not true?

I recently watched an episode of my favorite television show, *Biography.* (I'm starting to like this show even more than *COPS.*) This particular episode focused on the Rat Pack, with Frank Sinatra and his friends. These guys were famous singers of the 1950s and 1960s, and by the world's standards they had it all. But now, fifty years later, they're all dead: Peter Lawford, Dean Martin, Sammy Davis, Jr., Joey Bishop, and Frank Sinatra. Perhaps you're too young to have heard of these guys, but I can guarantee you your parents and grandparents recognize these names. As I watched the show I thought to myself, *Nothing really lasts without Christ. We may have everything the world can offer, but in the end it's nothing without Jesus.*

THE UNREPENTANT CRIMINAL

Each of these criminals faced a monumental choice when he looked at Jesus. The unrepentant man refused to submit to Jesus; instead, he hurled insults and mocked Him. He said, *Are You the Christ? Save Yourself and us!* Given his precarious position, this was cruel sarcasm, wouldn't you agree?

But someone may say, "Dawson, didn't this guy ask to be saved? Aren't those the magic words that get a person into heaven?" Yes, he did say, "Save me." Yet it's never about words alone, but rather the intent of the heart. It's obvious this criminal's cry for help was not out of submission to Christ; it was a selfish plea from a unrepentant man. Though he said the words *Save me,* we know he died an unsaved man. How do we know? Because Jesus never answered him. This man showed no fear of God whatsoever, no remorse for his sin. He knew he was going to die soon, yet he remained sarcastic, cold, and mocking.

Instead of responding to any conviction of the Holy Spirit, he remained disrespectful and defiant until the end. Thus, Jesus didn't answer him. Saying the "right" words doesn't get God's attention—God looks at the heart. Jesus didn't talk with this man.

The Bible tells us in Proverbs 1:28–29, "They will call to me but I will not answer; they will look for me but will not find me. Since they hated knowledge and did not choose the fear of the LORD" (NIV). Criminal number one never got through to Jesus Christ, and when he died he slipped into eternal hell.

Several years ago I was sharing my faith with a young punk on the streets of Los Angeles. He said, "Hey, man, I've prayed the prayer; I tried that 'blankety-blank' Jesus stuff and it doesn't work." He thought his four-letter words and his limited vocabulary would shock me. It didn't. I looked him straight in the eye and said, "Dingbat, zingbat, zook!" He said, "What?" I replied "Dingbat, zingbat, zook!" He said, "Hey, buddy, what does that mean?" I answered, "It means nothing, just like your prayer to Jesus, because you didn't mean it."

Friend, you can say all the words in the world, but if you don't have a broken and repentant heart before God, you simply won't get through. It doesn't work! Did you know that 94 percent of all Americans say they believe in God? Yet the world is not changed, and neither are many of their lives. Why? Because many people know about Jesus, but they have never met Him personally.

I once heard about a Russian guy who found a gospel tract, read about Jesus on the cross, then prayed, "God, You're a fine chap. If I were You and You were me, I wouldn't have died for You. Thank You." Presto—Christ came into his life and he was born again. Why? It wasn't because he got the words exactly right, but rather because his heart was right before God. God will always listen to a repentant heart.

THE REPENTANT CRIMINAL

As things progress, we find that criminal number two is a different story. This man becomes one of the greatest models of faith and allegiance to Jesus Christ in the entire Bible.

> But the other rebuked him and said, "Don't you even fear God since you're under the same punishment this Man is? We've been punished justly—we're receiving only what our actions deserve. But this Man did nothing wrong! Jesus," he said, "remember me when You come into Your kingdom." "I tell you the truth," Jesus answered, "today you will be with Me in Paradise." (Luke 23:40–43, 45a TGL, pp. 252–53)

So here's the question: What did this repentant criminal see or hear that caused him to give his life to Jesus

Christ? What moved him from insulting and mocking Jesus to the point of submitting himself to Christ's lordship? To me, this is one of the greatest pictures of faith in the Bible. In fact, I think he may have understood faith even better than the eleven disciples. What did he see in Jesus?

First off, he would have seen the inscription above Jesus' head: JESUS OF NAZARETH KING OF THE JEWS. This was written in three different languages, including Greek, which this man understood. This Jewish man must have been asking himself, Is it possible? Is Jesus really the King of our people, the promised Messiah? Maybe the sign got him thinking.

Or perhaps it was Christ's patience and silence. People mocked Jesus hour after hour. They abused Him, laughing at His nakedness, yet Jesus never said a word. Maybe this criminal, though fighting great pain, thought back to Isaiah 53:7 where it says, "He was oppressed and He was afflicted, yet He did not open His mouth; like a lamb that is led to slaughter, and like a sheep that is silent before its shearers, so He did not open His mouth" (NASB). Certainly, this must have made the criminal take notice.

Or maybe it was Christ's prayers for His enemies' forgiveness. As we mentioned earlier, Jesus would often push up and cry, *Father, give them another chance. Let them be.* Then He'd sink down again to catch His breath. When another throng of people passed by He would rise up again and say, *Father, give them a chance; they don't know what they're doing.* He was asking the Father to hold off His judgment.

Can you imagine what this thief was thinking as he watched Jesus in action? He must have thought, T*his is the real deal. I've never seen anything like this in all my life.* Again, he might have recalled the words from Isaiah 53 and Psalm 22, which describe the anticipated Suffering Servant. It could be his mother impressed these things on his mind as a boy, or that he remembered them from synagogue. The words from Psalm 22 might have been ringing in his ears as he watched Jesus:

> All who see me mock me;
> they hurl insults, shaking their heads:
> "He trusts in the LORD;
> let the LORD rescue him.
> Let him deliver him,
> since he delights in him." (Ps. 22:7–8 NIV)

These are the very words he was hearing from the rulers and crowds; he must have thought to himself, *This is no coincidence—this must be the Christ!*

THE APPROPRIATE RESPONSE

How do we know this repentant criminal was saved by Christ? For starters, we see him stand up and defend

Christ. Outside Pilate's initial response, he's the first one since the Garden of Gethsemane who has taken a public stand for Jesus. This man turned to his partner in crime and rebuked him, saying, *Stop it; stop it. Don't you even fear God, since we are under the same sentence? Don't you feel any terror about meeting God? We're going to die, and you're not even thinking about facing eternity!* He was shocked at the flippant attitude of his friend.

But he didn't stop there; he also confessed his own sinfulness. In front of the leaders, crowds, and soldiers, he took responsibility for his actions. He said to his friend, "We are punished justly; we are getting what our deeds deserve." This is an amazing statement. If you've spent time around prisons, you know they're full of people who won't admit their own guilt—it's always someone else's fault. Yet this man took full responsibility. He confessed his sin.

Finally, he recognized Jesus Christ for who He was. As far as we know, he'd never seen Christ's miracles or heard Him teach. Yet the Holy Spirit gave him absolute assurance that Jesus was the Messiah. So he turned to Christ and said, "Remember me when You come into Your kingdom." He doesn't say, *I want to sit on Your right or Your left,* or, *I want to be somebody big in Your kingdom.* His request is simple: *Just remember me, that's all. Please, just remember me.*

Oh, the humility and simplicity of it all. He believed Jesus would somehow raise him from the dead, to a place where Jesus would rule forever. Someone once wrote, *Some saw Jesus raise people from the dead, yet didn't believe; the thief sees Christ put to death, and yet believed.* Ironically, he recognized the suffering and dying Messiah to be the Author of Life. Thus, his simple plea: *Please, just remember me.*

CHRIST'S TENDER RESPONSE

What do you think Jesus felt when He heard the thief's words? This is the first time someone had ministered to Him since the angels in the garden. It must have greatly encouraged His heart. Some scholars believe a smile came across Christ's face at that moment: here was a sinner coming home, at the very last hour.

Jesus answered the thief—that's always a good sign. And Jesus said, "I tell you the truth, today you will be with Me in Paradise." In this one sentence there were three elements of good news. First, Jesus said, "Today." He didn't say "tomorrow" or "three days from now." Death by crucifixion would often last for days, but Christ's words assured the man his suffering would soon be over. Sure enough, three hours later the soldiers broke the legs of the two criminals, causing them to suffocate to death. It wasn't pleasant, but at least the suffering was ended.

Second, Christ was saying, *You're going to be with Me. Think of that. You don't need to be afraid, for the very moment you die I'll be right at your side.* The third assurance, though, was best of all: *You'll be with Me in Paradise* . . . a place of joy, of beauty, of peace. *You'll be with Me in Paradise* . . . What a beautiful promise from Jesus Christ.

THE GREAT DECISION

Here were two men . . . one on either side of Jesus. Both started at the same place, yet one entered hell and the other heaven. Let me ask you: which criminal do you want to be? Criminal number one remained defiant and rebellious, and he now faces an eternity apart from God in hell. Criminal number two became broken before God in humility, and Jesus promised him entrance into eternal life. Take your pick—which criminal do you want to be?

You may say, "Dawson, I want to be like criminal number two; I want to be the man or woman God wants me to be, and go to heaven when I die." Then tell that to God. Tell Him you know you're a sinner, you need Him to forgive your sins, and you need Him to control your life. Let Him know that you're grateful He paid for your sins on His cross.

The Bible says, "Choose this day whom you will serve" (Josh. 24:15 ESV). I pray, my friend, that you will choose Christ.

10

A Cry Out of the Darkness

Friday, 3:00 p.m.–6:00 p.m.

We've now come to Christ's final hours on earth. His face is set like flint to do the Father's will. Yet Jesus is continually caring for others, even at the height of His own pain and suffering. From the cross He looks through the tiny slits of His beat-up eyes and sees His mother, Mary, standing before Him. What pain must have creased her face as she watched her precious son suffering. Jesus, having cared for the needs of the repentant thief, now turns to care for His mother.

> Standing by the cross of Jesus were His mother and His mother's sister, as well as Mary the wife of Clopas and Mary Magdalene. When Jesus saw His mother and the disciple whom He loved standing nearby, He said to His mother, "Woman, here is your son." Then He said to the disciple, "Here is

> your mother." From that moment on, this disciple took her into his home. (John 19:25–27 TGL, p. 253)

It's difficult for us as fallen, finite people to grasp how Jesus could reach out to others while in His weakened, tortured condition. We've seen Him pray for those who crucified Him, and grant forgiveness and hope to the repentant thief. Now, in a spirit of great tenderness and sensitivity, Jesus ignores His pain and makes final arrangements for His mother.

The example Jesus gives in this act is both touching and remarkable. Ladies, if you're dating a guy and you're curious as to how he'll someday treat his wife, just watch how he treats his mother. You can tell a lot about a guy's spiritual life by how he treats his mom. Some guys might say, *But Dawson, you don't understand. My mother is* (as we used to say in my day) *"full weird." I don't know what's going on with her hormones, but I'm paying for it! Besides, she's just not in touch with where I'm at—when I'm under the most pressure she can make things difficult for me. How dare you test my spirituality by how I treat my mother!* Agree with me or not, I still think it's true. Jesus loved His mother and took care of her to the end.

DARKNESS FALLS

Now the scene changes dramatically. Though the sun is high in the sky an odd thing happens—God turns out the lights. The city of Jerusalem becomes engulfed in darkness; we're talking pitch black. Why? Here's my theological thought, though others may differ. I believe that as God turned out the lights, He was making a statement about the overwhelming darkness His Son was about to face. As painful and tragic as were the first three hours on the cross, I believe Christ was now facing what He dreaded most. During the first three hours, God allowed humankind to pour out its full fury on Jesus. Now, it was God's turn to pour out His holy, hot displeasure (often referred to as wrath) upon His Son. The first hours were no picnic, but the worst was yet to come.

In the Bible darkness is a symbol of sin, hell, and judgment. In fact, during Jesus' ministry He told a parable about a man who ended up in hell: "The king said to the servants, 'Bind him hand and foot, and throw him into the outer darkness; in that place there will be weeping and gnashing of teeth'" (Matt. 22:13 NASB).

Hell is described as "outer darkness," for it will be pitch dark. I'm sure you've heard people say, *It's okay if I go to hell because all my friends are going there too; we're going to have a party.* Wrong! You cannot have a party when you can't see your hand in front of your face; nor can you party when you're in constant pain and torment. You may say, *Dawson, I've been in pain before.* Perhaps, but have you gnashed your teeth because of pain? That's the picture we're given of hell.

In some mysterious way, I believe that Jesus Christ

stepped into a literal hell during His last three hours on the cross. I say this for several reasons. Number one, the Bible tells us He was covered with filth. Second Corinthians 5:21 states, "He made Him who knew no sin to be sin on our behalf, so that we might become the righteousness of God in Him" (NASB). Jesus, in some way, actually became sin. If I were to ask you, "Who's the greatest sinner who ever lived?" what would you say? Some would say Mao Tse-tung, who killed at least thirty-five million people; others would say Stalin, who starved millions to death on purpose. Hitler would also come to mind. But no, the greatest sinner who ever lived was Jesus Christ as He hung upon that cross. All of humankind's sins—past, present, and future—were laid upon Him at once. This includes yours and mine as well.

Can you imagine the shock this would have been to Jesus Christ? He had lived a sinless life—absolutely perfect in every way. He had never committed the tiniest of sins; yet now sin covered Him, and mysteriously wove its way into His very identity.

You and I can't fully relate, but let me illustrate a portion of how it felt to Jesus. During World War II Josef Mengele, an infamous Nazi leader, ran the concentration camps in Germany. His usual procedure was to separate small children from their parents as they arrived at the camps by train. The children were often killed first, followed by senior citizens. Middle-aged adults were kept alive only if they were strong enough to perform hard labor.

As you can imagine, parents would desperately try to hold on to their children during this terror-filled process.

The story is told of a family unloaded off the train at a certain camp, the parents clinging to their baby. Mengele had the children ripped from the parents' arms, but as they resisted he grabbed the baby and cut the child in two with his sword. He then tossed a piece of the child to each parent, saying, "See, there's your baby!"

I can't think of anything more horrible. Yet God is so pure that a white lie to Him is like Mengele to you and me, only multiplied billons of times. The holiest being that has ever existed, Jesus Christ, suddenly stepped into hell. All the sins of the world were poured upon Him—He bore the full responsibility and guilt. Can you imagine how He must have felt? How terrifying this must have been.

To add to His suffering, Jesus felt profound loneliness for the first and only time in all eternity. There have always been perfect love and fellowship among the members of the Trinity—Father, Son, and Holy Spirit. Our God has never experienced loneliness, for He is utterly perfect and complete in who He is. Therefore, He's never been in need of someone, or something, to satisfy Him or make Him complete. He lacks nothing, including the joy of community and fellowship within Himself.

It's hard to imagine, isn't it, that this perfect union among the Father, Son, and Holy Spirit was broken in an instant. How hard this must have been for Jesus; how painful for the Father and the Holy Spirit. They were now obligated to treat the Son as the worst sinner in all of history. Friends, as difficult as was Christ's physical suffering, His spiritual suffering was far worse. The bearing of God's wrath in our place is what makes the Cross so beautifully tragic.

Several years ago I spoke at a youth camp out west. One of the employees enforced the rule that anyone who broke camp guidelines would be swatted with the oar from a rowboat. It was called "getting the swats." Believe me, this was years ago.

Of course, one of the kids at camp got into trouble, so the employee called the boy and me in for a chat. "Dawson," he began, "this kid is in trouble; we're going to have to give him the swats." This particular kid had had a difficult childhood, and I knew "the swats" would be counterproductive. I told the employee no, that it wasn't going to happen.

"Then we're going to send him home from camp," he responded. I reached into my pocket, pulled out the keys to my Volkswagen (which was held together by Jesus stickers), and threw them to the boy.

The employee sent the boy out of the room. "No, hey, wait a minute. We can't really send him home—he's not old enough to go alone. I don't think, though, you understand the real issue here. A rule's been broken, and in order to maintain order and discipline here at camp, somebody has to get the swats. Somebody broke the law."

I said, "Well, then, I'll take the swats."

The employee looked at me for a moment, then said, "Dawson, you and I are friends, right?" I agreed. "Well," he continued, "just because we're friends doesn't mean I can go easy on you." I assured him I was aware of that, and then went outside to explain our decision to the boy. Big tears came to this rough kid's eyes and dripped down his cheeks. "No, Dawson," he said, "I'll take the swats." Of course, I looked toward heaven and whispered, *Thank You, Lord.* And that's what happened—the boy took his punishment.

You see, back before the beginning of time, the Father, the Son, and the Holy Spirit must have had a conversation that set up the plan of the ages. The Father might have said, "I am holy—I hate sin!" The Son and the Holy Spirit would have agreed. Then the Father might have said, "All sin must be punished." Again, the Son and the Holy Spirit would have agreed, acknowledging that every wrong must be dealt with, every sin must be punished. Every one!

Then, evidently, Jesus stepped forward and said, "Father, if You have to pour out Your wrath on someone, let it be Me." In other words He was saying, I'll take the swats! Friend, please hear me on this. Someone's going to pay for the sins you've committed. You can accept the fact that Jesus paid the price for your sins on the cross, or you can pay the penalty yourself (an eternity apart from God). The fact is, somebody will *take the swats.*

PAYING OUR DEBT

So here is Jesus Christ experiencing God's wrath in our place. I believe during these last hours on the cross He was sucked down into the black hole of hell. It may have felt to Him as if He would stay in hell forever. And here's the real mystery: Christ had to suffer enough in those three hours to pay for every person's sin, for all of eternity. Now figure that out!

But there He was, deep in the black hole, being sucked further and further into the back side of darkness and hell. Picture Him trying to get through to the Father, quietly praying, His lips barely moving due to agony (see His prayer in Psalm 22). He's praying, *God, please, I know You are holy; I know Our forefathers cried out to You and were delivered, yet I'm praying with no answer. I'm as nothing but a worm before You.* Imagine the desperation, the suffocating pressure of God's wrath upon His chest. He's trying to get through to the Father, but it appears the Father isn't listening; His judgment is like none other in all eternity. The separation from His Father threatened to undue Him . . . threatened to abandon Him to complete isolation from all things holy. Finally, after three long hours, feeling as if He's on the very edge of being eternally forsaken, He cries out to the Father with a loud yell, "My God, My God, why have You left Me behind?"

And bam! . . . it was over. God grabbed Him from the back side of the darkness and pulled Him to His bosom—the victory was won, right then and there! The wrath of God had been satisfied for all who would receive salvation as a free gift. Sin had been paid for, once and for all.

IT IS FINISHED!

> When some of those who were standing there heard it, they said, "Look, this Man is calling for Elijah." And now Jesus, knowing that everything was accomplished, said the words, "I am thirsty" in fulfillment of Scripture. A jar of sour wine was sitting there, and one of the men ran to it at once. He took a sponge, filled it with the wine, put it on a hyssop stalk, and lifted it to Jesus' mouth. "Let Him drink," he and the others said. "Let's see if Elijah comes to take Him down and save Him." (Matt. 27:47–49; Mark 15:35–36; John 19:28–29 TGL, p. 253)

The crowd that was standing by the cross misunderstood Jesus' anguished call. They thought He was calling out to Elijah to help Him. A Jewish tradition taught that Elijah would come before the Messiah and introduce the Messiah to the people. The hardened crowd at the cross thought it was some kind of joke that Jesus would be calling out to Elijah at such a time as this.

"After taking the wine, Jesus again cried out in a loud voice, 'It is finished!' Then He bowed His head. 'Father,' He said, 'into Your hands I commit My spirit.' After saying these words, He yielded up His spirit and breathed His last" (Matt. 27:50; Mark 15:37; Luke 23:46; John 19:30 TGL, pp. 253–54).

Alive for a few more moments, Jesus turned to the soldiers and said, "I thirst." He was offered a sponge filled with sour wine, just enough to loosen His dry and swollen tongue. Then He yelled out in victory, *"It . . . is . . . finished!"* This English phrase is actually one word in the original language—Tetelestoi. It was often used to describe the idea of being paid in full, or that of "perfect completion."[1] People would use this word to describe something so perfect that nothing could be added to it. When an artist had a perfect drawing he would say, "Tetelestoi." Or when a debt was paid in full, the one who loaned the money would say, "Tetelestoi."

At this moment in world history, Jesus yells out for all to hear, "Tetelestoi!" In other words, *I came to this world that people might have new life, and have it abundantly; I came so that people would never have to walk in fear and guilt again; I came so that people might have life in heaven for all eternity, and I've done it all. I did it! I did it! Tetelestoi!* Then, having completed the work the Father sent Him to do, Jesus surrendered His spirit and died.

WHAT DOES IT MEAN?

Of course, the story doesn't end with Jesus on the cross. Three days later He was raised from the dead, and He now lives in a glorified body. No power on earth, whether Annas, Caiaphas, Pilate, or Satan himself, could keep Jesus from rising again. The Resurrection declares that Jesus Christ is God. We can't see Him or touch Him, but someday we will. He's alive, and now He offers a simple question to every person on earth: *What will you do with Me? It's your decision now. What will you do with Me?*

Friend, do you want to deal with the Lord? Do you want to find this Christ we've been following to, and through, the Cross? Do you want your life changed? You say, *Dawson, this story is really exciting, I know. I've read the book and seen the movie. It's a good story.* Yes, and that's all it will be, unless you embrace its meaning and apply it to yourself.

This God who loves you desires to be at the center of your life, for now and for eternity. As you've encountered Jesus Christ on His walk to the Cross, perhaps you've felt a tugging in the pit of your stomach, something that makes you want to become a follower of Jesus. If that's the case, it's not something you ate, but rather the Holy Spirit speaking to you. I would encourage you to surrender to this desire and follow God by embracing His Son.

It may be that you're already religious. In fact, you may be the leader of a church board or the president of your church youth group. These are good things, but if you've never accepted Christ into your heart, they mean nothing. Your daddy may be the best deacon your church has ever seen, but his faith won't get you to God. You've got to deal one-on-one with the Lord Jesus Christ.

Some say, "But Dawson, I go to church; I've even been baptized." Friend, going to church doesn't make you a Christian any more than going to the pizza parlor makes you a pizza. And being baptized doesn't make you a Christian any more than jumping in a bathtub makes you an Olympic swimmer. Church and baptism are important, but by themselves they can't change our sinful hearts. Only Christ can do that.

How does this happen? What must take place for a person to become, as Jesus called it, "born again"? Actually, it's quite simple. You must humble yourself before a perfect God and recognize His divine right to your life. (We'll look at this more closely in chapter 18.)

It may be you've already received Christ; if so, that's wonderful. But some who read these words are Christians living a life that breaks God's heart. Jesus didn't die on the cross for you to willfully continue in sin. He wants you to enjoy His victory in your life, living moment-by-moment by the power He supplies. Christian, if you're living a life of willful disobedience to God, I implore you to turn back to Him.

It doesn't matter who you are or what you've done. Jesus Christ walked His painful journey to the Cross for your sins and mine. Let's live for Him, working and waiting for the day when we'll be with Him forever. Praise God, His walk to the Cross has made this possible.

II

The Restoration of Peter

The dramatic story of Peter wouldn't be complete without observing his restoration by Jesus after the Resurrection. Though Peter had failed his Lord miserably, Jesus went to great lengths to personally care for His broken disciple. By doing so, Christ revealed the tender mercies and forgiving heart that are of such great benefit to all His followers.

Early on Sunday morning, an angel appeared to several of Jesus' followers: "'Don't be alarmed,' he said. 'You are looking for Jesus the Nazarene, who was crucified. He has risen! He is not here. See the place where they laid him. But go, tell his disciples and Peter, "He is going ahead of you into Galilee. There you will see him, just as he told you."'" (Mark 16:6–7 NIV)

A PERSONAL ANNOUNCEMENT

How did Jesus go about restoring Peter? First, He had the angels at the empty tomb announce that Christ wanted to meet Peter in Galilee. Perhaps you'll remember that the first ones to find the tomb empty were Mary Magdalene, Mary the mother of James, and Salome. They had brought spices with which to give Jesus' body a proper burial. Imagine their surprise when they saw the stone in front of the tomb rolled to the side, an angel sitting in its place. The Bible says simply, "They were alarmed" (Luke 16:5 NIV).

It was a miracle that Christ was risen from the dead! How shocking it must have been to hear the angel announce that Jesus was no longer there. To the frightened and bewildered women, he added a command: "But go, tell his disciples and Peter, 'He is going ahead of you into Galilee'" (Luke 16:7 NIV). It couldn't have been clearer; Jesus wanted to reunite with Peter and the disciples, and this would take place in Galilee.

Why did Jesus say "Peter, and the disciples"? What was the point of singling out Peter by name? I believe Jesus knew Peter was more devastated and crushed over his sin than most of us can imagine. Peter had clearly repented of his sin, yet he would still have to face his fellow disciples, all of whom knew about his treacherous denials. Therefore, Jesus knew Peter needed a special word of encouragement; Peter needed to hear that Christ wanted to see him.

Also, Jesus was expressing to Peter and the disciples His great love and acceptance for them. Barclay wrote, "It was characteristic of Jesus that He thought, not of all the wrong Peter had done Him, but altogether of the remorse that Peter was undergoing. Jesus was far more eager to comfort the penitent sinner than to punish the sin. Someone has said, 'The most precious thing about Jesus is the way in which he trusts us on the field of our defeat.'"[1]

A PERSONAL ENCOUNTER

Late on Sunday afternoon Jesus appeared to two men as they traveled to the city of Emmaus. These men were walking along, discussing the events of the previous few days, when a stranger appeared to them and asked what they were talking about. This stranger joined the conversation, teaching about the Messiah from the Old Testament Scriptures. It was the most beautiful explanation of God's plan they'd ever heard—it made their ears burn with excitement. The Man suddenly disappeared, and immediately the travelers knew they'd been talking with the risen Jesus. Thrilled, they ran back to Jerusalem to tell the disciples of their experience. Yet before the men could share their story, the disciples exclaimed, "It is true! The Lord has risen and has appeared to Simon" (Luke 24:34 NIV).

Evidently, Jesus had found Peter earlier in the day. No one outside God and Peter knows what took place during that very personal encounter. Maybe God kept it out of the Bible because it was so sacred. I can imagine, though, there must have been tears, confession, and brokenness on the part of Peter. As for Jesus, He surely spoke words of love, forgiveness, and encouragement to His hurting disciple.

Though we don't know what was said, we do know it was Jesus' top priority to meet with Peter before meeting with the other disciples. The apostle Paul later recalled the sequence of Christ's appearances: "He was buried, . . . he was raised on the third day according to the Scriptures, and . . . he appeared to Peter, and then to the Twelve. After that, he appeared to more than five hundred of the brothers at the same time, most of whom are still living, though some have fallen asleep" (1 Cor. 15:4–6 NIV).

Even though Peter had failed Jesus miserably, he was still a top priority to the risen Christ.

A PERSONAL RESTORATION

> When they had finished eating, Jesus said to Simon Peter, "Simon son of John, do you truly love me more than these?"
>
> "Yes, Lord," he said, "you know that I love you."
>
> Jesus said, "Feed my lambs."
>
> Again Jesus said, "Simon son of John, do you truly love me?"

He answered, "Yes, Lord, you know that I love you."

Jesus said, "Take care of my sheep."

The third time he said to him, "Simon son of John, do you love me?"

Peter was hurt because Jesus asked him the third time, "Do you love me?" He said, "Lord, you know all things; you know that I love you."

Jesus said, "Feed my sheep." (John 21:15–17 NIV)

Now, days later, we watch as Jesus restores Peter to public ministry. It takes place in Galilee, around a campfire on the banks of the Sea of Tiberias. Jesus cooked breakfast for several of the disciples, then invited Peter for a short walk. Peter had denied his Lord three times; now he's given three opportunities to affirm his love for the Savior. In this very intimate setting, Jesus turned to Peter and said, "Simon, son of John, do you love Me more than these?"

Jesus wanted to know if Peter truly loved Him. In the original language Jesus used the word *agape* for "love," meaning, *Peter, do you love Me with the greatest kind of love*[2]*—the kind of love I have for you? And, do you love Me more than the other disciples do?*

Peter's answer showed he'd learned humility. He responded by saying, "Yes, Lord . . . You know that I love You." However, the word Peter used for "love" was *phileo,* meaning "brotherly or affectionate love."[3] Peter refused to say he loved Jesus more than the others. One commentator wrote: "This man is through boasting. Never again will he brag of what he will do. Never again will you hear him saying, 'I am going to do something big for the Lord.' From here on he is going to do something big, but he is not going to say anything about it. He comes to the low plain: 'I have an affection for You.'"[4]

Jesus' response was to give Peter a challenge: "Feed my lambs." This was a huge responsibility. By commanding Peter to feed His lambs, Jesus was saying, *Take care of My most precious possessions—those who will come to Me as new believers and need special care.*

Jesus then asked, "Peter, do you truly love Me?" Jesus dropped all comparisons, no longer asking Peter if he loved Christ more than others. He wanted to know if Peter had *agape* love for Him. He was saying, in essence, *Peter, let's forget any comparisons with others, for you no longer believe you're better than everyone else. But Peter, do you love Me with* agape *love?*

In his newfound humility, Peter could not tell Jesus he loved Him with *agape* love. He knew in his heart the most he could offer was *phileo,* or brotherly love. Peter didn't yet understand that *agape* love comes only through the Holy Spirit. The New Testament teaches this in Romans 5:5: "Hope does not disappoint us, because God has poured out his love [*agape*] into our hearts by the Holy Spirit, whom he has given us" (NIV).

Yet Jesus, instead of belittling Peter for not having

agape love for Him, entrusted Peter with even more responsibility. He said, "Take care of My sheep." Jesus was asking Peter to take care of and discipline those who believed in Him and had become mature in Christ. This meant Peter himself would need to mature, to assume more responsibility than he'd ever imagined.

Amazingly, Christ asked Peter a third question, saying, "Do you love Me?" This was a question of tremendous love and compassion, for now Jesus uses the word *phileo* rather than the word *agape.* In other words, Jesus was asking Peter, *Do you at least have brotherly love for Me?* In His kindness Jesus was willing to accept whatever love Peter could offer Him. When Peter heard this, however, his heart was broken. "Peter was hurt because Jesus asked him the third time, 'Do you love me?' He said, 'Lord, you know all things; you know that I love you'" (John 21:17 NIV).

One writer explained Peter's response this way:

> It was as though Peter was saying, "You know I have personal affection for you. You know me through and through. You know everything. You know what I said and what I did and what I am. You know me better than I know myself. Lord, out of all your knowledge of me you know I have brotherly love for you. You know I love you (phileo) and I know I can never love you the way you love me (agape)." It was the confession of a man who had been put to the wall by his conscience and

> who stood now before the Lord, broken, aware of his weakness, sensitive to his limitations, and afraid to ever boast again.[5]

Jesus didn't berate Peter for his lack of *agape* love. Instead, He entrusted Peter with even more responsibility. By doing this He showed Peter He had more trust in him than ever. Jesus' final command was "Feed my sheep." Again, He was asking Peter to feed mature Christians. This was no small task. As an apostle, Peter would need to study God's Word and know its deep meaning in order to help mature believers grow and continue in the faith.

LESSONS TO LEARN

For those of us who fail (and that's all of us, by the way), Peter's story of denial and redemption should bring great encouragement and hope. Though Peter was rightly humbled, he became one of the greatest leaders for Christ of all time. He led the early church with great humility and passion. And, it's worth noting, there came a time when Peter proved his *agape* love for his Savior. Jesus had told him:

> "Most assuredly, I say to you, when you were younger, you girded yourself and walked where you wished; but when you are old, you will stretch out your hands, and another will gird you and

> carry you where you do not wish." This He spoke, signifying by what death he would glorify God. And when He had spoken this, He said to him, "Follow Me." (John 21:18–19 NKJV)

Church tradition tells us Peter did follow Christ from that point on, both faithfully and powerfully. Gone were the arrogance and untempered strength that had caused him to fail his Lord so treacherously. In its place were brokenness and humility, allowing him to lead Christ's sheep with wisdom and compassion. As for his death, Jesus' words proved true. As an old man, Peter was crucified in Rome for his faith, on a wooden cross, upside down. Such was the *agape* love God worked into Peter's life. The belligerent, loudmouthed fisherman from Galilee was changed forever by the personal love and mercy of Jesus Christ. By God's grace, may it change us as well.

12

A Great Encounter

In order to fully appreciate Christ's walk to the Cross, we must also enter into the joy of His resurrection. We've watched the risen Lord deal gently with His broken disciple, Peter. Let's now examine His encounter with another of His followers, Mary Magdalene. She has much to teach us about loving devotion to Christ.

Mary Magdalene's story is one of faith and heartbreak, fear, confusion, and absolute despair. Yet it concludes with unbelievable joy and triumph. She had watched her beloved Savior suffer and die, yet her devotion didn't stop when He was placed in the tomb.

> But Mary stood outside the tomb crying. As she wept, she bent over to look into the tomb and saw two angels in white, seated where Jesus' body had been, one at the head and the other at the foot.

They asked her, "Woman, why are you crying?"

"They have taken my Lord away," she said, "and I don't know where they have put him." At this, she turned around and saw Jesus standing there, but she did not realize that it was Jesus.

"Woman," he said, "why are you crying? Who is it you are looking for?"

Thinking he was the gardener, she said, "Sir, if you have carried him away, tell me where you have put him, and I will get him."

Jesus said to her, "Mary."

She turned toward him and cried out in Aramaic, "Rabboni!" (which means Teacher).

Jesus said, "Do not hold on to me, for I have not yet returned to the Father. Go instead to my brothers and tell them, 'I am returning to my Father and your Father, to my God and your God.'"

Mary Magdalene went to the disciples with the news: "I have seen the Lord!" And she told them that he had said these things to her. (John 20:11–18 NIV)

THE MOMENT OF MEETING

Mary Magdalene was truly blessed, for she encountered Jesus Christ at perhaps the greatest moment in all of history: the Resurrection! In order to understand who she was, let's take a quick look at this dear follower of Christ. Mary "the Magdalene" received her name from her birth town of Magdala. This small town was located just three miles from Capernaum, and was known for its primitive textile factories and dye works. It also had a history of prostitution, which leads most to believe she'd been a prostitute before she met Christ. Ancient Jewish scholars referred to a "Miriam Megaddela," which literally meant "Mary with the braided locks." In that time a woman would not braid her hair unless she lived a sinful lifestyle.[1]

Whether she'd lived in promiscuity or not, we do know she was possessed by seven demons prior to meeting Jesus. The Bible tells us of "Mary Magdalene, out of whom he had driven seven demons" (Mark 16:9 NIV). Thus, her life must have been saturated with the lust, bitterness, hatred, and despair that would naturally come from a heart filled with evil.

After her deliverance, Mary's gratitude and devotion led her to join a group of women who followed Jesus from town to town supporting His ministry. What Jesus said of a different woman described Mary as well: "I tell you, her many sins have been forgiven—for she loved much. But he who has been forgiven little loves little" (Luke 7:47 NIV). Jesus had radically transformed her life, and she devoted herself to Him and His teaching.

The Gospel writers, when referring to these women followers of Christ, often listed Mary's name first. Perhaps she'd earned a special respect due to her age and her lifestyle of devotion. In fact, the early church leader Saint Augustine gave Mary Magdalene the title "the Apostle of the Apostles" because she was the first to see the risen Christ.

A TRAIL OF TEARS

With great devotion, however, came great suffering. Let's follow, for a moment, Mary Magdalene's trail of tears:

Friday

2:00 a.m.	Christ was taken from the Garden of Gethsemane to Annas's apartment where He was questioned. (John 18:12–24)
3:00 a.m.	Christ appeared before the Sanhedrin and Caiaphas. (Matt. 26:57–68)
5:00 a.m.	Christ was sentenced to die by the Sanhedrin for blasphemy. (Luke 22:66–71)
5:30 a.m.	Pilate questioned Christ, then sent Him to Herod. (Luke 23:1–7)
6:30 a.m.	Herod questioned Christ, then returned Him to Pilate. (Luke 23:8–11)
7:30 a.m.	Pilate sought to release Christ, had Christ beaten, then sent Him to be crucified. (Matt. 27:15–26; Mark 15:6–15; John 19:1–16)

9 a.m.–Noon	Mary Magdalene and the entire crowd watch the sufferings of Christ on the cross. (Mark 15:22–32)
Noon– 3:00 p.m.	Darkness covered the land. (Matt. 27:45)
3:00 p.m.	Mary Magdalene and the true followers of Jesus stood by helplessly as Christ spoke His last words and died. (Luke 23:46; John 19:28–30, 34–37)
Late Afternoon	Joseph of Arimathea claimed Christ's body. He and Nicodemus prepared it for burial. Christ's body was laid in Joseph's new tomb. It was there that Mary Magdalene followed them to the gravesite and witnessed the stone being rolled in front of the tomb. (Matt. 27:57–61; Mark 15:42–47; John 19:38–42)
Saturday	Early afternoon and into the evening, Mary Magdalene and the ladies mourned the death of their Savior and prepared spices in order to preserve His body. Late that evening they awaited the morning journey to the sepulcher.

One can only imagine the heartbreak Mary suffered during the hours after Christ's death. Jewish law prohibited anyone from traveling during the Sabbath. Therefore, she and all the followers of Jesus stayed in their houses and mourned His tragic death—His promised resurrection was far from their minds.

Early on Sunday morning things appeared even worse for Jesus' followers:

> Early on the first day of the week, while it was still dark, Mary Magdalene went to the tomb and saw that the stone had been removed from the entrance. So she came running to Simon Peter and the other disciple, the one Jesus loved, and said, "They have taken the Lord out of the tomb, and we don't know where they have put him!" (John 20:1–2 NIV)

We've looked at the time line of Jesus' trials and crucifixion; let's now review the events that surrounded His resurrection:

- About 5:00 a.m. Mary Magdalene, along with Mary the mother of James and Salome (and perhaps some others), set out for the tomb. It was still dark, but dawn was near. Mary Magdalene hurried on ahead of the others, found the tomb open, and ran to tell Peter and John.
- About 5:30 a.m. the other women arrived. By this time the sun was up (Mark 16:2). They saw an angel who sent a message to the disciples (Matt. 28:5; Mark 16:5).
- About 6:00 a.m. another group (among whom was Joanna) arrived at the tomb (Luke 24:1; Mark 16:1). They

saw what they took to be "two young men" who gave them words of comfort and instruction (Luke 24:4).

- About 6:30 a.m. Peter and John came to the tomb. Mary Magdalene evidently followed them, but did not go home when they did. She saw two angels. About the same time the other women delivered their marvelous news to the other disciples (Luke 24:10).
- About 7:00 a.m., the Lord revealed Himself to Mary Magdalene (John 20:14–18; Mark 16:9). Not long afterward he revealed Himself, it would seem, to the company of women who by this time were returning to the tomb. They were charged by the Lord with a message to His disciples to meet him in Galilee (Matt. 28:9).[2]

THE SOUND OF WEEPING

We pick up the story at Mary's second visit to the empty tomb. The first sound we hear is that of intense weeping. Just when Mary Magdalene thought she could mourn no more, she discovered a whole new depth of grief. It appeared something horrible had happened—someone had stolen Jesus' body. "Mary stood outside the tomb crying. As she wept, she bent over to look into the tomb" (John 20:11 NIV). When she looked into the tomb, she saw something incredible: "[Mary] saw two angels in white, seated where Jesus' body had been, one at the head and the other at the foot. They asked her, 'Woman, why are you crying?' 'They have taken my Lord away,' she said, 'and I don't know where they have put him'" (John 20:12–13 NIV).

Though she didn't understand the significance of these two angels, their very presence gave evidence something wonderful had happened. The angels were dressed in white, signifying the very holiness and purity of God, a symbol of the heavenly world.[3] The Bible tells us the angels were "seated," with "one at the head and the other at the foot" of where Christ had lain. This would have drawn attention to the grave clothes left behind, further evidence that the body wasn't stolen. Here the angels sat, peacefully and quietly waiting for Mary Magdalene, ready with the amazing news of His resurrection.

A PROBING QUESTION

Mary must have been speechless as she peered into the tomb. The angels spoke first, asking her a simple yet deeply probing question: "Woman, why are you crying?" (John 20:13a NIV). It was a question designed to gently but firmly help her gain control of her emotions. It's as though the angels were lovingly implying, *There really is no reason for you to be sobbing at all.* In fact, the opposite was true—this was a time for rejoicing as never before. The evidence of the miraculous was all around her: the empty tomb, the shining angels, the way the grave clothes were untouched—all of this confirmed Jesus' prediction that He would rise on the third day.

We might expect that Mary would be overjoyed and amazed at the sight of all these things. But she was far too single-minded, driven by her grief and unbelief. She answered the angels by saying, "They have taken my Lord away . . . and I don't know where they have put him" (John 20:13b NIV).

Poor Mary! She'd come to the tomb to anoint the dead body of Jesus, to be near Him in His death. She was hoping to find some closure for her grief. Instead, she's even more devastated by the empty tomb. Despite the evidence, she remains convinced someone has stolen Jesus' body, and it compounds her grieving.

HER QUESTIONS ANSWERED

The angels might have responded to Mary's fears, but there was no need. They could see, standing directly behind her, the One for whom she was searching. "At this, she turned around and saw Jesus standing there, but she did not realize that it was Jesus" (John 20:14 NIV). Perhaps she turned around because of something she saw in the angels' eyes, we don't know. But as she turned, she failed to recognize her risen Lord.

Why did she fail to recognize Jesus? There are several possible answers to this question. Perhaps her eyes were filled with tears, blurring her vision. Or maybe the vivid memories of Jesus' bruised and broken body, still fresh in her mind, kept her mind closed to the fact He was standing before her. It's also possible she was supernaturally prevented from recognizing Him at that moment, similar to the experience of the two men on the road to Emmaus. Whatever the reason, she wasn't prepared to see Him alive, and her mind refused to accept the truth.

Jesus asked Mary, "Woman . . . why are you crying? Who is it you are looking for?" (John 20:15a NIV). In her grief and confusion, she assumed this man was the gardener. "She said, 'Sir, if you have carried him away, tell me where you have put him, and I will get him'" (John 20:15b NIV). Being early in the morning, and also a holiday (Feast of First Fruits), she reasoned the only person in the garden at that time would be the gardener. *If he works here, maybe he knows where they've taken Jesus' body.* And so with deep love, she inquired as to His whereabouts.

One writer said this of Mary's plea: "How true is the proverb 'Love feels no load.' Jesus was in the prime of life when he was crucified, and had a hundred pounds weight of spices added to his body; and yet Mary thinks of nothing less than carrying him away with her, if she can but find where he is laid!"[4]

Mary had a false hope. She thought the best that could happen was to find the dead body of Jesus Christ. Her inability to find Him caused her to weep. But praise God she didn't find what she was looking for! If she'd found the dead body of Jesus, the world would be found weeping for all eternity!

WEEPING TURNS TO JOY

The time had come for Jesus to open the eyes of this loving but confused follower. "Jesus said to her, 'Mary.' She turned toward him and cried out in Aramaic, 'Rabboni!' (which means Teacher)" (John 20:16 NIV). It took but one word from the lips of Jesus to end her incredible confusion: "Mary." She became convinced of the Resurrection not by her eyes, but by her ears.

Perhaps Jesus had spoken to Mary in a similar tone when He drove the seven demons from her (see Luke 8:2). Maybe she recognized His tone from when He'd spoken to His mother from the cross (see John 19:26). Regardless, she heard the voice she loved above all voices. Jesus called out to her in her native Aramaic tongue, "Miriam."

By this one word she was lifted from sunken grief to ecstatic joy. Mary called to Jesus, "Rabboni," which literally means "my Master." This was a term of both endearment and respect. Her risen Lord, her Teacher, was standing before her, and she fell at His feet. As she lay on her face before Him she must have grabbed His feet, for He said to her: "Do not hold on to me, for I have not yet returned to the Father. Go instead to my brothers and tell them, 'I am returning to my Father and your Father, to my God and your God'" (John 20:17 NIV).

It seems like an odd response from Jesus, doesn't it? Mary was hanging on to Him for dear life. By her actions she was saying, *You're back, alive! I refuse to let You go! Life will now be as it was.* Yet Jesus, direct and full of love, refused to let her cling to Him. Yes, He was alive, but there were things she needed to understand, and she no longer needed to fear His loss. In essence He was saying, *You'll never lose Me again, Mary. But My relationship with My followers will be different now. Tell My disciples what you've seen.*

LESSONS LEARNED

What a morning this had been for Mary Magdalene. She'd gone from agonizing grief to ultimate joy and celebration. Her devotion to Christ on that Sunday was evidenced by her loving actions:

- She was one of the last to leave His cross.
- She was the first to the tomb.
- She was the first to tell anyone of the empty tomb.
- She was the only one alone at the tomb.
- She was determined to find His missing body.
- She was willing to take care of His body alone.

Because of her great devotion, Mary Magdalene was rewarded by Christ:

- She was the first to see the risen Christ.
- She was the first to talk to the risen Christ.

- She was the first to touch the risen Christ.
- She was the first to hear of His new plans.
- She was the first to be given the responsibility of telling others of Christ's plans.

How beautiful is the devotion of Mary Magdalene! Her trail of tears led through deep sorrow and pain, followed by miraculous joy. Her life is an example for us today. She teaches us that all who follow Christ will join in His sufferings, yet also share the joy of His resurrection. "Mary Magdalene went to the disciples with the news: 'I have seen the Lord!' And she told them that he had said these things to her" (John 20:18 NIV).

PART II

A CLOSER LOOK

In the first part of this book, you and I have carefully walked with Jesus Christ to the cross of His suffering. It's been a fascinating and sorrowful journey, hasn't it? A journey filled with awe at His love and endurance—a journey filled with pain as we watched Him lay down His life for our good.

This kind of love not only humbles us, but it leaves us with many questions as well. Why did Jesus Christ endure such hostility for our sake? What caused Him to drink to the dregs the cup of suffering the Father put before Him? To understand His motives fully would be to understand the mind of God—something we'll never fully achieve. However, elsewhere in the New Testament—in the letter to the Philippians—the apostle Paul gives us insight into the humbling steps Christ took in order to redeem humankind. In a sense, it's a behind-the-scenes view of what sent Jesus on His journey to the Cross.

Come with me, then, as we journey even deeper into the mystery of Christ's passion, as revealed in Philippians 2:5–11:

> Have this attitude in yourselves which was also in Christ Jesus, who, although He existed in the form of God, did not regard equality with God a thing to be grasped, but emptied Himself, taking the form of a bond-servant, and being made in the likeness of men. Being found in appearance as a man, He humbled Himself by becoming obedient to the point of death, even death on a cross. For this reason also, God highly exalted Him, and bestowed on Him the name which is above every name, so that at the name of Jesus every knee will bow, of those who are in heaven and on earth and under the earth, and that every tongue will confess that Jesus Christ is Lord, to the glory of God the Father. (NASB)

13

He Made Himself Nothing

Paul wrote, "Your attitude should be the same as that of Christ Jesus: Who, being in very nature God, did not equate equality with God something to be grasped, but made himself nothing" (Phil. 2:6–7a NIV).

In this profound passage we learn that Jesus Christ willingly traveled from great riches to great rags, and was then rewarded with even greater glory. It's my prayer that as we study Christ's walk to the Cross by way of this passage, we will fall more deeply in love with Jesus Christ. It's impossible to love someone we don't know, isn't that true? That's why when people fall in love, they spend great amounts of time with each other. They want to learn about the other person—their likes, dislikes, past history, and future dreams. It's my intent that through this passage we'll enjoy that same desire to know Jesus Christ in a deeper way.

Here's the big thought behind Christ's first step down: He did not regard equality with God a thing to be grasped. He let it go. And beyond this, the Bible tells us Jesus "made himself nothing" (Phil. 2:7a NIV), or, as some translations say, He "emptied Himself" (NASB). This is one of the greatest phrases in the Bible. In fact, we can't fully understand Jesus Christ until we wrestle with this phrase. Also, if we don't come to a correct understanding of what this means, we'll find ourselves believing some bad theology. Let's explore, then, this very difficult subject.

HE EMPTIED HIMSELF

In Philippians 2 the apostle Paul talks of the incredible humility and sacrifice of Jesus Christ. We're told that Jesus, who is forever God—with all the rights and privileges of being God—emptied Himself. What does this mean? Certainly, different people have different ideas. While studying this passage I decided to check a sermon site on the Internet, to see what various people had to say. I found that many commentaries skip right over this verse, it's so deep. In fact, one commentator said, "This expression 'he emptied himself' is so profound that scholars have tried in vain to plumb its depths."[1]

As I see it, trying to understand this phrase is like trying to plumb the depths of the ocean. I've heard that no one has ever been able to reach the deepest part of the ocean's floor, which in some areas is seven miles deep.

At times scientists will lower small robots with cameras attached, but the pressure is so great it blows them apart. Of course, deeper down still is the earth's crust, then the mantle, and finally the earth's core. Has anyone ever been to the core of the earth? Of course not, but I'd say we have a greater chance of making it to the core of the earth than we do of completely understanding this small phrase: "He emptied Himself."

Just because we can't understand it fully, however, doesn't mean we shouldn't explore it as best we can. The Greek word for "emptying" is *kenow,*[2] and when scholars talk of this passage they often refer to it as the "kenosis passage." It can be defined in this way: "to make void, or make of no reputation."[3] It also has the idea of "eliminating all the privileges or prerogatives associated with such high status or rank."[4] Can anyone have a higher rank than Jesus Christ? Never. The prophet Isaiah, when foretelling Christ's birth, referred to Him as "Wonderful Counselor, Mighty God, Eternal Father, Prince of Peace" (Isa. 9:6 NASB). The Bible makes clear that Jesus is God—completely equal with the Father. Jesus did not cease being God when He came to earth—rather, He laid aside the privileges and prerogatives of His deity during His earthly mission.

When someone becomes president of the United States, does that person receive perks and prerogatives with his high rank? Of course he does. One example is the use of *Air Force One,* the presidential airplane. This plane has one of the most elaborate communication systems in the world. It has a beautiful bedroom in the back, and gorgeous offices in the front. And wherever it travels, it's accompanied by squadrons of fighter jets. What a great perk! Also, the president has full use of the White House with all its luxuries, history, and antiques. The president gets to enjoy these things every day—they're perks that go along with the job.

What if the president one day decided to travel cross-country, but in a 1972 Volkswagen Bug instead of *Air Force One?* If you're my age, you'll remember that Volkswagen "Bugs" had a whopping fifty-two horsepower engine, no air-conditioning, and a heater that consisted of two squirrels in the engine compartment rubbing sticks together. If the president did this, he'd be giving up his perks, right? In a small, silly way, he'd be doing what Jesus did on a much grander scale; he'd be "laying aside" the prerogatives that were rightfully his.

Jesus Christ, fully and always God, did not quit being God when He came to earth. Rather, He "laid aside" the perks for a while. In looking at different translations of the Bible, some express this thought by saying He "made himself of no reputation" (Phil. 2:7 KJV). And what a reputation He had, as Creator of the heavens and the earth. Amazingly, He made Himself of zero reputation.

Many years ago, at the age of twenty-five or twenty-six, I was a pure visionary. I didn't really know what I was doing, but I had a dream, and that was to create a late-night music program on secular TV. Way back in the seventies there was a show called *Midnight Special,* a late-night music program; this was pre-MTV, if you can believe it. My idea was to create a show that would immediately follow *Midnight Special,* thus giving me a chance to share the gospel. So we set to work and somehow made twelve shows. But when it came time to produce twelve more, I was forced to go and raise more money. Incredibly, I found a man who was interested in financially backing the project.

I was so excited I came home and told all my friends that we had the money. I then jumped into my Volkswagen Bug and traveled throughout the country, visiting television stations. Sure enough, we found twenty-five stations that would air our show for free. Then I went back to the man in order to get his large donation. When we sat down, I found he'd decided to donate his money to another religious organization.

I was livid—absolutely furious! And I wept with angry tears! Shortly afterward I was with my father, and in anger I took a pillow and threw it against the wall. I said, "I've got a question for you, Dad. Why doesn't God pay His bills?" (It's only by God's grace I wasn't struck dead by a lightning bolt!) My dad looked at me and said, "Son, you're worried about your reputation, aren't you? You told all your friends you had the money, and now you're embarrassed. Let me remind you that Jesus made Himself of no reputation. God will pay His bills on time."

Of course, my dad was right. I was embarrassed—concerned for my own reputation. But Jesus was willing to give up His reputation for our sake. I love how different translations and paraphrases of the Bible quote Philippians 2:7: The New International Version says that He "made himself nothing"; *The Message* says, "He set aside the privileges of deity"; *The Living Bible* says that He "laid aside his mighty power and glory." So let me combine all these translations in order to help us grasp what this passage is saying: *He gave up His place with God and made Himself nothing; He laid aside His might and power and glory and the privileges of His deity, and impoverished Himself; in fact, He made Himself of no reputation.*

Okay, you may be saying, *He did all this; He made Himself nothing, He impoverished Himself, He laid aside the privileges of His deity and His power and His glory. But how did He do it, and what exactly does this mean?*

Before we can answer that question, we must first understand what He did *not* lay aside during His mission to earth. That is, He never, ever emptied Himself of His deity. Ever. At no time did He cease to be God. The Bible tells us that one of God's attributes is His immutability. That means He never changes. The prophet Malachi, in the Old Testament, quoted God by saying, "I am the LORD, I do not change" (Mal. 3:6 NKJV). In the New Testament book of Hebrews we read, "Jesus Christ is the same yesterday and today and forever" (13:8 NASB). Jesus Christ has always been God; He always will be God. So when He walked this earth He was, yes, God.

If Jesus didn't stop being God, of what did He empty Himself while on this earth? In order to illustrate, let's say the best basketball player in the NBA came to a local high school and said to the principal, "I'd like to put on a display for your student body. And I'd like you to choose your school's best player for me to play against. But here's the deal: I'm going to tie weights to my ankles, and tie my shooting hand behind my back." Do you get the picture? He's choosing to lay aside the privileges of his rank and ability. Though he may do these things in order to slow himself down, he's still an NBA star.

HIS GREAT GLORY

What, then, are the privileges that Jesus laid aside? Let me list a number of things that are readily apparent. First, He emptied Himself of His great glory. *Glory* means "brilliance, splendor or radiance."[5] In the Bible, glory is often signified by a bright light. Imagine the blinding brilliance of Jesus Christ in His eternal, pre-incarnate state. He was forever brilliant.

I would imagine that all of us, at one time or another, have been in our own glory. What does that mean? I have a friend named Don who is a gifted musician. He has the ability to take familiar songs and arrange them beautifully. He first teaches the choir to sing their individual parts. Then he works with the orchestra—the flutes come in here, the horns come in there, the violins play in this manner. By the time he's done, he's created—in genius fashion—a beautiful work of art. Now imagine Don onstage at Carnegie Hall, leading choir and orchestra in a great performance unto God. The choir breaks into a beautiful song that he found and arranged; the orchestra kicks in and it takes your breath away. People are in awe, and when Don turns and bows to the audience, everyone stands and applauds. At that very moment, Don is in his glory.

As a communicator I have been in my glory. Several years ago I was the keynote speaker at an evening rally attended by fifteen thousand college students. The auditorium was so dark, and the lights so bright, that I couldn't see a single person in front of me—not one. But I could feel the crowd. It was one of those evenings when God took over, and I literally felt as though I was standing back and watching Him work. When I gave the altar call at the end of my talk, students streamed down the aisles for a full fifteen minutes in order to commit their lives to Christ. As an evangelist and youth communicator, at that moment I was in my glory!

It's not wrong to be in one's glory, because Jesus Christ, for all eternity past, was in His own glory. In fact, we get a glimpse of the pre-incarnate Jesus in Isaiah 6:3, where the angels cry out, "Holy, Holy, Holy, is the Lord of hosts, the whole earth is full of His glory" (NASB). The brilliance of it all! Jesus shone so brightly no man could lay eyes on Him and live. You may remember in Exodus 33–34, when Moses climbed up the mountain and said, "God, I want to see You." God's reply was, "Moses, no man can see Me and live." Moses, however, wouldn't give up, so finally God hid Moses in between some rocks, passed by him, and then allowed Moses to see the aftermath of His glory. In other words, He allowed Moses to see His fumes. When Moses came down off the mountain, his face shone so brightly he had to cover it with a veil. Now that, folks, is glory.

When Christ came to earth He laid aside His wonderful, brilliant glory in order to become the son of a carpenter. He was ignored and misunderstood, hated and ridiculed, rejected and put to shame. It's no wonder He prayed to His Father, "Glorify Me together with Yourself, with the glory which I had with You before the world was" (John 17:5 NASB). He was ready to go home and pick it up again. All this time the angels must have been shaking their heads at what Christ had done. The supreme Creator of the universe had laid aside His glory in order to redeem sinful man.

JESUS' GREAT RICHES

Not only did Jesus lay aside His glory; He also emptied Himself of His great riches. How rich is Jesus? That's kind of a nonsense question, isn't it? We could never calculate the net worth of Jesus Christ. He merely spoke and creation happened. He can forever keep creating, and thus add to His net worth if He so desires. For example, He told His disciples, "If I go and prepare a place for you, I will come again and receive you to Myself" (John 14:3 NASB). Jesus has been creating heaven, I believe, for two thousand years. How rich is Jesus? Well, how much is heaven worth?

In Philippians 4:19 we're told, "My God will meet all your needs according to his glorious riches in Christ Jesus" (NIV). "Glorious," as in splendid, eye-catching, and full of renown. There are very rich people who live in magnificence and splendor, but the richest person in the world is a pauper compared to Jesus Christ. Think of Bill Gates, who is worth $50 to $90 billion on any given day. He makes $6 billion a year on interest alone. In comparison to Jesus Christ, how rich is Bill Gates? He doesn't even show up on the welfare level.

Look what God said to the children of Israel: "I have no need of a bull from your stall . . . for the world is mine, and all that is in it" (Ps. 50:9, 12 NIV). The real question shouldn't be "How rich is Jesus?" but rather, "How poor did He become?" Jesus went from infinite riches to absolute poverty; a greater drop than we'll ever know. The apostle Paul wrote in 2 Corinthians 8:9, "You know the grace of our Lord Jesus Christ, that though he was rich, yet for your sakes he became poor, so that you through his poverty might become rich" (NIV).

THE POVERTY OF JESUS

How poor was Jesus? He was so poor that He was forever borrowing from those around Him. Remember, He wasn't born in a hospital or a hotel room, but in a smelly animal's pen. They put Him out with the animals, and He was laid in a feeding trough. As a grown man He never had a house of His own. He could never say to His disciples, "Hey, guys, let's go hang out at My place." Instead He told them, "Foxes have holes and birds of the air have nests, but the Son of Man has no place to lay his head" (Matt. 8:20 NIV). Truly, Jesus was homeless as He walked this earth.

What else didn't He have? He didn't have a building from which to preach. When He was teaching by a lake and the crowd pressed in on Him, He borrowed Peter's boat so He could teach from off shore. When He taught at the temple or in a synagogue, it was always on borrowed time. He wasn't the pastor of some four-columned church with the benefit of an expense account. He was dependent upon others for their help.

Who paid for Jesus to walk this earth? Who put up the money? Amazingly, it was a bunch of women who bankrolled Jesus' ministry—something not well-received in those days. Luke 8:1–3 says:

> Jesus traveled about from one town and village to another, proclaiming the good news of the kingdom of God. The Twelve were with him, and also some women who had been cured of evil spirits and diseases: Mary (called Magdalene) from whom seven demons had come out; Joanna the wife of Cuza, the manager of Herod's household; Susanna; and many others. These women were helping to support them out of their own means. (NIV)

Can you imagine someone listening to Jesus, then turning to his buddy and saying, *I wonder who's supporting this Man? What, a bunch of women? Oh, brother—isn't He ashamed of that?* Again, in that day it would have been scandalous.

What about His transportation? He entered Jerusalem on a borrowed donkey. How about the last supper He ate with His disciples? He had to borrow a room for that. The only possessions Jesus owned were the clothes on His back and the sandals on His feet, and even these were taken from Him as He hung on the cross. In fact, Jesus hung naked on the cross for the entire world to see. People stared at Him and made fun of His nakedness, which is sexual abuse. No matter what you've been through, Jesus understands.

Last, Jesus had no tomb in which to be buried. A man named Joseph of Arimathea placed Jesus in his own tomb. Otherwise, Jesus' body would have gone to the city dump, where animals would have torn it to pieces.

Friend, it's impossible for us to fully grasp that Jesus Christ "emptied Himself" of His rights and privileges as God. We stand in awe of the One who gladly laid aside His glory and riches to rescue us from the penalty of our sin. This is the Jesus who walked to the Cross on our behalf.

May we be eternally grateful.

14

He Laid Aside His Glory and Riches

As we have seen, no one can comprehend all that Christ sacrificed by becoming a man. Yet we know He took unimaginable steps down when He "emptied Himself" of His divine rights. In the previous chapter we examined this truth, and though we can't understand its full depth, we do know Jesus laid aside many of the perks and privileges that come with being God. We learned that He emptied Himself of His brilliant glory, as well as His infinite riches.

As we continue to examine this passage in Philippians, Christ's next step is to empty Himself of the expression of His deity: He "emptied Himself, taking the form of a bond-servant, and being made in the likeness of men" (Phil. 2:7 NASB). Can you imagine how difficult it was for Jesus to conceal His deity while on earth? It's true He clearly taught He was equal to the Father, and thus was

God. Also, His life fulfilled every one of the Old Testament prophecies concerning the coming Messiah. Yet, except for the miracles He performed on various occasions, His deity remained obscure.

When Jesus became Man, He added to Himself the "excess baggage" of human nature. Jesus is more than God in a body. The Bible teaches that Jesus Christ added full humanity to His deity. In other words, Jesus added a human nature to His already existing divine nature. From His birth, and now for all eternity, Jesus remains one Person with two distinct natures. He is the perfect God-man, Jesus Christ. This is what theologians (those who study God and His ways) call the "mystery of the Incarnation." So, Jesus emptied Himself of not only His great glory and infinite riches, but also the expression of His deity while on earth.

THE GOD WHO REVEALS

God has always wanted to reveal Himself, is that not true? In fact, He is constantly revealing Himself through nature, through His Word, through providence, and in many other ways. Why? Because this is the greatest thing He can do for us as humankind—to reveal Himself. One time a student came up to me and said, "I think God's on a big ego trip—all He did was create us humans so that we'd worship Him." I was shocked by his statement, but God gave me the answer right away. I said, "Listen, God's not on an ego trip—He's on a love trip! God is so great, His love is so great, His creativity is so great, His ways are so great, that out of His great love for us He created us to enjoy Himself forever." No, God didn't make us because He needed us, or because He's an egomaniac. He created us because He is love—so that we might enjoy Him forever!

I once attended a play that depicted the story of Creation. As it began a guy got up as narrator and said, "God was very lonely so He said, 'I will make man in My own image.'" God was lonely? Baloney! God has never been lonely except for the occasion when Jesus, on the cross, bore our sins on Himself and thus experienced separation from the Father. At that point Jesus cried, "My God, My God, why have You left Me behind?" And all heaven wept. It's the only time in all eternity when God Himself has tasted loneliness.

Jesus, though fully God, walked this earth wrapped in a robe of human flesh. For a God who loves to reveal Himself, this must have been hard going. As an illustration, think of women in the Middle East who wear a burka, or a full-body garment with a head covering. Due to world events you and I see pictures of that region on a daily basis, don't we? In those pictures we often see women going about their daily lives completely veiled. To me, that seems like a difficult thing, especially considering the heat of the Middle East. Even if a woman is very beautiful, with a lovely complexion and beautiful hair, she can't reveal herself in public. She is completely covered, often from head to toe.

In a sense, Jesus walked this earth in a burka. It wasn't a burka of cloth, but one of human flesh. How very humbling this must have been, having to cloak the full expression of His deity. There were, of course, occasions when Jesus would give people a glimpse of His divine nature. In the Gospels we often see the humanity and deity of Jesus revealed side by side. It's almost as though He chose to lift the veil for a moment or two, then quickly lowered it to continue His mission. As you can imagine, this often made His disciples greatly confused.

HUMANITY AND DEITY TOGETHER

Consider how you would have reacted to some of Christ's words and actions. For instance, in Matthew 24, when Jesus spoke of His second coming (as the Son of God—deity), He told His disciples that no one knows the day or the hour, but only the Father; not even the angels or the Son (humanity). In other words, *I am the Son of God, but I don't know when I'm coming back.* Wait a minute—He is God, but He doesn't know all things? As we used to say in the 1980s—go figure!

Here's another story that shows the humanity and deity of Jesus side by side. Jesus gets in a boat with His disciples and crosses a lake. Without warning a serious storm comes up, with waves crashing over the boat. But Jesus, exhausted from all the ministry He's been doing (humanity), stays asleep in the back of the boat. He'd been teaching and healing and casting out demons all day, and was asleep even though the boat was about to sink. The disciples were so afraid they woke Jesus up. Jesus, after rebuking them for their small faith, then rebuked the wind and the sea. Immediately things became still. No wind, no waves; only perfect calm. This is deity. The disciples were amazed and now very confused, and they asked one another, "Who is this, that even wind and sea obey His command?" (Mark 4:41 TGL, p. 92).

Another example is when Jesus raised Lazarus from the dead. That would be deity, right? Lazarus had been dead for four days, and when Jesus arrived Lazarus's sister Mary approached Him, saying, "'If You had been here my brother would not have died.' When Jesus saw both her and the Jews weeping, He sighed deeply and was troubled. 'Where have you laid him?' He asked. 'Lord, come and see,' they answered. Jesus wept" (John 11:32–35 TGL, p. 178).

Look at the humanity involved in Jesus' question, "Where have you laid him?" Jesus was about to raise His friend from the dead, and He said, *Hey, by the way—where's the body?* I don't believe this was a mental game Jesus was playing with His disciples—He really didn't know where Lazarus's body was. Of course, they led Him to the tomb, Jesus called Lazarus out of the grave, and we see this great act of deity alongside His simple humanity. Amazing.

Finally, I think of Jesus on the cross, talking with the repentant thief. He said to him, "Today you will be with me in Paradise." (Deity.) Then He looked down at the crowd and through blurry eyes saw Mary and said to her, "Mother." (Humanity.)

My question to you is this: Do you think it was easy for Jesus to wrap His deity in a burka, better known as a human body? It was never easy, but He did it because He loved us and was willing to suffer deep humiliation in order to save us.

UNDER THE FATHER'S AUTHORITY

We've learned that Jesus emptied Himself of His riches, His glory, and the full expression of His deity. But there's more. He also laid aside His independent authority as God, placing Himself under the authority of the Father. Jesus has always been fully equal with God and the Holy Spirit. Together they complete the Trinity, the three-in-one Godhead. Yet when Jesus emptied Himself and became a man, He put Himself completely under the authority of the Father and yielded Himself fully to the leading of the Holy Spirit. As a man He learned how to trust the Father for everything, becoming the first and only human to walk totally by faith.

If anyone ever asks you, "Who is the person in the Bible who most walked by faith? Was it Abraham, or Moses, or even Paul the Apostle?" No, only one person has walked by faith His entire life, without failure—the God-man, Jesus Christ. As our example, He placed Himself under the authority of the Father and the leading of the Holy Spirit. This is a mystery. Theologians call this Christ's "humbled state."

Why was Jesus willing to trust the Father for everything? Because He knew the Father, that's why. He knew the Father would never let Him down. He trusted Him even to the point of death on a cross. What keeps you and I from trusting God fully? Ultimately, it's the sin of pride, isn't it? Our pride tells us we know better than God how to run our lives. Do you know the biggest lie Satan has ever told humankind? It's this: *Dependence upon God is death; independence from God is life. Do your own thing; be your own God.* This is a lie from the pit of hell, and when Jesus walked this earth He put that lie to rest. He was totally dependent upon God the Father, all the way to dying on the cross. It's no wonder the Father has given Him a name that is above every name. At the Cross and the Resurrection, Jesus laid bare Satan's lies. In order to accomplish this, He humbled Himself before the Father.

Let's look at some examples of this from Scripture:

- In John 4:34, the disciples were going to bring Jesus food for lunch, but Jesus said, "My food . . . is to do the will of him who sent me and to finish his work" (NIV).
- In John 5:19 Jesus told His disciples: "I tell you the truth, the Son can do nothing by himself; he can do

only what he sees his Father doing, because whatever the Father does the Son also does" (NIV).

- In John 5:30 He says, "By myself I can do nothing; I judge only as I hear, and my judgment is just, for I seek not to please myself but him who sent me" (NIV).
- Jesus is quoted in John 14:28 as saying: "You heard me say, 'I am going away and I am coming back to you.' If you loved me, you would be glad that I am going to the Father, for the Father is greater than I'" (NIV).

The Jehovah's Witnesses, who deny Christ's claims to deity, use these same verses to deceive people. They say that Christ is not God—that He's not equal to the Father. They use these verses out of context. Fortunately, we have the entire Bible, Old and New Testaments, by which we discover the humanity and deity of Jesus Christ. Verses like these show us that Jesus humbled Himself completely. He emptied Himself of the use of His independent authority and placed Himself under the authority of the Father.

BECOMING A BONDSERVANT

The Bible says Jesus humbled Himself even further. Christ continued His humbling steps down by placing Himself under the authority of man. Philippians 2:7 says He took the form of "a bondservant" (NKJV). The word for "bondservant" in Greek is *doulos,* which means "a slave or someone devoted to another, to the disregard of one's own interests."[1] In Christ's day you couldn't get any lower than a slave. It was the very bottom of the ladder. Yet Jesus lowered Himself to this level—He became a bondservant, a slave to the slaves.

Can you believe this? Jesus went from King of kings to slave of slaves. He became like us so we could become like Him. Jesus came to serve, and He often told His disciples about His mission of service: "Who is greater, the one who is at the table or the one who serves? Is it not the one who is at the table? But I am among you as one who serves" (Luke 22:27 NIV). As a bondservant, Jesus gave up His most basic rights: the right to spend time as He wished; the right to self-protection; the right to freedom of movement. Jesus gave it all away; He put Himself under the authority of both God and man. In doing so He suffered the indignities of man's sin, selfishness, and indifference. And yet He remained a humble servant to the end.

By God's grace, over many years on the radio I have talked to thousands and thousands of teenagers. Recently I did a show on sexual abuse, a nightmare in this twenty-first century. Statistics tell us one out of three girls in this country have been sexually or physically abused by the time they're nineteen. For guys, it's one out of six.[2] I've seen only one other violation that's tougher on a child, and that's when a mother abandons her children. Sexual abuse is not solved easily—it can lead to anxiety, depression, and many other problems. Christ came to save the lowest of the low, both those who have sinned and those who have been sinned against.

In this life we'll never comprehend all that Christ sacrificed when He "emptied Himself" and became a man. We'll never know how hard it was for Him to veil His deity in human flesh. We'll never completely fathom how He put Himself under the Father's authority and became servant of all humankind. Yet His humility and love should inspire us to become more like Him. What a wonderful Savior.

15

He Took on Humanity

Up to this point we've watched Jesus Christ take these humbling steps down the ladder of ultimate humility: He didn't consider equality with God a thing to be grasped, so He made Himself nothing. Second, He laid aside His heavenly perks and prerogatives and became a bondservant, a slave of all slaves.

Let's continue by examining Jesus' next step on the path to humility: "And being made in the likeness of men. Being found in appearance as a man, He humbled Himself by becoming obedient to the point of death, even death on a cross" (Phil. 2:7–8 NASB).

The apostle Paul, in one simple phrase, spoke volumes about the sacrifice Christ made. He said Christ was "made in the likeness of men." The Greek word for "made" means "come into existence." The word *likeness* means "that which is made to be like something else, not just in appearance, but in reality."[1] In other words, He didn't come as a clone, an angel, or a ghost; He was truly a man.

TRULY HUMAN

Jesus Christ was human in every way. He added not only a human nature to His divine nature, but a human body as well. But what kind of body did He have? Did He take on a body like Adam and Eve had before their sin against God? No. Did He take on a resurrection body like the one He now enjoys? No. Jesus took on a body like yours and mine. It was a body both judged and weakened, the result of man's sin. The Bible speaks of the struggles of our judged bodies:

> In the same way, our earthly bodies which die and decay are different from the bodies we shall have when we come back to life again, for they will never die. The bodies we have now embarrass us for they become sick and die; but they will be full of glory when we come back to life again. Yes, they are weak, dying bodies now, but when we live again they will be full of strength. (1 Cor. 15:42–43 TLB)

When Christ came to earth He inhabited a body just like ours. He became like us in every way. The Bible tells us: "For this reason he had to be made like his brothers in every way, in order that he might become a merciful and faithful high priest in service to God, and that he might make atonement for the sins of the people" (Heb. 2:17 NIV).

Jesus experienced many of the same emotions and physical struggles that we face daily. You and I came into the world through our mothers—so did Jesus. We needed the care and attention of our parents as we grew up—so did Jesus. We become tired, weak, hungry, thirsty, and sleepy. We are tempted by sin, and we sometimes feel sad, angry, and lonely. Jesus experienced all these things. And one day you and I will experience a physical death, something Jesus also experienced in His human body.

THE SAME, YET DIFFERENT

Yes, Jesus was fully human. But thankfully He was different from us in one very important aspect: He was without sin. The Greek word for "likeness" stresses similarities, yes, but also leaves room for differences. In Hebrews 4:15 we're told, "We do not have a high priest who is unable to sympathize with our weaknesses, but we have one who has been tempted in every way, just as we are—yet without sin" (NIV).

You and I are selfish, proud, and often indifferent to God—Jesus wasn't. We struggle with laziness, impure thoughts, jealousy, and materialism—Jesus didn't. That's why His enemies became frustrated—they couldn't find sin in His life of which to accuse Him. They truly hated Him for this, leading Jesus to ask, "Which of you can truthfully accuse me of sin? And since I am telling you the truth, why don't you believe me?" (John 8:46 NLT).

Jesus lived a perfect and holy life, though surrounded by the ravages of sin. The Bible speaks of a man in the Old Testament named Lot, who suffered because of the sins he saw daily: "He rescued Lot, a righteous man, who was distressed by the filthy lives of lawless men (for that righteous man, living among them day after day, was tormented in his righteous soul by the lawless deeds he saw and heard)" (2 Pet. 2:7–8 NIV). If Lot suffered in the midst of a wicked society, Christ suffered all the more. He was "made in the likeness of men," yet without sin.

IN MAN'S APPEARANCE

And now a further step down. The Philippians passage tells us Jesus was "found in appearance as a man." The Greek word for "found" means "to recognize,"[2] and the word for "appearance" means "the outward shape or form."[3] Thus, when Jesus walked from village to village most people formed their opinion of Him based on outward appearance only. There was nothing about His features that would lead people to believe He was more than an average-looking, peasant Jew. The prophet Isaiah spoke of this hundreds of years before: "He has no stately form or majesty that we should look upon Him, nor appearance that we should be attracted to Him" (Isa. 53:2 NASB).

Think of it! What if God walked by you at the mall and you didn't recognize Him? Or He sat next to you at Starbucks and you had no idea? That's what happened to the people of His day; He walked among them, yet most of them were clueless. How humbling this must have been for Jesus, especially in His own hometown:

> All spoke well of Him and were amazed at the gracious words that came from His lips. "Isn't this Joseph's son?" they asked . . . "I tell you the truth," he continued, "no prophet is accepted in his hometown . . ." All the people in the synagogue were furious when they heard this. They got up, drove him out of the town, and took him to the brow of the hill upon which the town was built, in order to throw him down the cliff. But he walked right through the crowd and went on his way. (Luke 4:22–30 NIV)

Yes, Jesus Christ is one of a kind. Fully God, He added to Himself a human nature and walked this earth in obscurity and humility. Earthly kings announce their greatness, yet Jesus took steps to hide His glory. Yet, as we'll see in the next chapter, He stooped even further. His humbling steps were not yet complete.

16

He Died a Horrible Death

By studying Philippians 2:5–11, we are gaining insight into Jesus' painful walk to the Cross. In a sense, God is pulling back the veil, allowing us to see the humiliating steps Jesus took on His way to the Cross. In this chapter we'll explore the remaining two steps that Jesus took.

JESUS HUMBLED HIMSELF

In Philippians 2:8 we learn that Jesus now entered the very depths of humility—He reached bottom by the act of dying a horrible death: "Being found in appearance as a man, He humbled Himself by becoming obedient to the point of death, even death on a cross" (NASB).

It's as though Jesus descended to the bottom of a bottomless pit. The word for "humbled" in the Greek language literally means "to lie low."[1] Jesus continued to the deepest depths of humility. He had His eyes set on the Cross, and nothing was going to stop Him.

I remember learning back in junior high about the Irish Republican Army, a violent Catholic group that was waging war against Protestants and the English army. I learned about some men, caught up in the conflict, who decided to make a political point by starving themselves to death. They were led by a man named Bobby Sands. I don't know if you've ever fasted, but it's amazing what happens to the body when deprived of food. For the first couple of days it screams out, "I am stomach . . . hear me roar!" By the third day the stomach shrinks, and though weakness sets in, things become bearable. This continues until forty days have passed; then things become dangerous.

Bobby Sands and his friends were guarded by the IRA, and the nightly news began to cover their progress. Day after day I'd watch Walter Cronkite report on their condition, and it was terrible. At day fifty Bobby Sands went blind. I remember thinking, *Why doesn't somebody stop this guy?* No one did, however, and on day fifty-six of his fast, Bobby Sands died.

I tell this story to illustrate how the angels must have felt as they watched Jesus sink lower and lower toward death. *Will somebody please stop Jesus Christ from doing this? It is so hard to watch,* they must have said to one another. Peter tried to stop Jesus, didn't he? In Matthew 16:22–23 he turned to Christ and said, "'Never, Lord. This shall never happen to you!' Jesus turned and said to Peter, 'Get behind me, Satan! You are a stumbling block to me; you do not have in mind the things of God, but the things of men'" (NIV). There was no one who could stop Jesus from humbling Himself to death. Jesus wouldn't allow it! No one could deter Him from the mission He'd set out to accomplish.

ANOTHER STEP DOWN

Now Christ lowers to another step very, very quickly; it's as if He's in a free fall. The Bible tells us He suffered the ultimate humiliation by "becoming obedient to the point of death" (Phil. 2:8 NASB). This was another step of humiliation, friends, that is beyond our description. What does it mean that He became obedient to the Father? It means He put Himself under the Father's authority by making obedience His total life commitment. Yet the cost is more than we could ever fathom.

Author Dwight Edwards wrote this concerning Christ's sacrificial obedience:

> We have now seen Christ's mindset go from the zenith of equality with God to the depths of humiliation. He left His splendor and privileges in heaven to come to this sin infested earth. Naked He was born, despised by men; naked He died

> despised by men. He did not just give up most of what was His, He gave up everything. His entire life was lived in the shadow of a cross, each step bringing Him nearer to the ultimate in shameful deaths.[2]

To be truthful, it was the Father's will that Jesus should die. You may say, "Dawson, are you making this up?" Not at all—it's in the Scriptures. Hebrews 10:9–10 says, speaking of Christ, "'Here I am, I have come to do your will.' . . . And by that will, we have been made holy through the sacrifice of the body of Jesus Christ once for all" (NIV). It was the Father's will that Jesus should die a sacrificial death on the cross. And Jesus was fully obedient.

Let me ask you, what is the greatest sacrifice you've made for Christ? I'll tell you mine, though I'm a bit embarrassed because it seems so superficial. For me it's traveling. I started on the road, speaking to teenagers, in 1972. I've stayed in fancy hotels and some that looked like bomb shelters. After a while they all look alike. I love doing ministry, but I've come to hate the travel involved.

A few years ago, at a board meeting, I met with the director of our ministry and said, "Monne, all I want to do is study two to three days a week, do research, and then get on the radio on Sunday nights. I don't want to do more traveling." His reply? "Dawson, we're going to work it out so you don't have to travel anymore." I thought I'd died and gone to heaven. It's like the old saying goes, *It's not the years, boys, it's the miles.* You may say, "Dawson, that's quite a sacrifice you've made—traveling for all those years." No, it isn't—not really. Not when compared to Christ and His sacrifice on the cross.

EVEN TO THE POINT OF DEATH

So Christ makes the right choice. He humbles Himself, becoming obedient "even to the point of death." This is the outer limits of humiliation. He obeyed, knowing it would take Him beyond unspeakable agony. Early in this book I asked the question "How hard was it for Jesus to die?" You know what? It's hard to die—it's a terrifying thing.

How hard was it for Jesus to die? I'm here to tell you Jesus Christ hates death. The only thing He hates more is sin itself, the cause of death. You say, "Dawson, do you have any proof of that?" Let's head back once more to the tomb of Lazarus. This friend of Jesus had been dead for four days, and Jesus was soon to raise him from the dead. Look at John 11:32–35:

> When Mary reached the place where Jesus was and saw him, she fell at his feet and said, "Lord, if you had been here, my brother would not have died." When Jesus saw her weeping, and the Jews who had come along with her also weeping, he

> was deeply moved in spirit and troubled. "Where have you laid him?" he asked. "Come and see, Lord," they replied. Jesus wept. (NIV)

Jesus was upset, even angry at what He saw—death and the suffering it caused. He understood that Satan brought death. He was enraged against the enemy—death—and the one behind the enemy: Satan. Death caused Jesus to weep and groan in agony.

How hard was it for Jesus to die? Now, of course, we are into mystery. Though He hated death, He willingly accepted it. He's the only man, ever, who's had the choice to either accept or reject death. No ordinary person has that choice, for all of us have sinned, and "the wages of sin is death" (Rom. 6:23 NIV). I once read about a popular singer and actor who on his deathbed was enraged that he had to die. That runs deep in all of us, doesn't it? Yet Jesus, being sinless, chose to accept the cold and cruel experience of death on the cross, even though He didn't have to.

Sometimes I wonder how often Jesus got alone with the Father, pleading with Him about His upcoming death. We just don't know. Some scholars say this happened only once, in the garden, but I personally believe it was far more than that. Look what it says in Hebrews 5:7: "During the days of Jesus' life on earth, he offered up prayers and petitions with loud cries and tears to the one who could save him from death, and he was heard because of his reverent submission" (NIV).

Just a week prior to His crucifixion, the horrors of His soon-coming death were felt as never before. Look at His words in John 12:27–29:

> "Now my heart is troubled, and what shall I say? 'Father, save me from this hour'? No, it was for this very reason I came to this hour. Father, glorify your name!" Then a voice came from heaven, "I have glorified it, and will glorify it again." The crowd that was there and heard it said it had thundered; others said an angel had spoken to him. (NIV)

Oh, heaven must have stood, the angels must have given a standing ovation, and the Father must have been so moved He couldn't keep silent. It was as if the Father was saying, *Hang on, Son. It's going to be worth it.* Jesus followed the Father's will even though it led through death.

One day a couple of Vietnam veterans told me stories of when they'd fought in the war. They described the terror of walking on jungle paths deep in enemy territory. One guy said, "We'd have these young sergeants come in without much experience. Trying to prove their worth, they'd take us right down a main path, which in the jungle is like a death sentence. It was a stupid thing to do." His buddy, standing next to him, said, "Yeah, and a lot of them got it in the back, too." Then he stopped, the two guys looked at each other, and not another word was spoken. I don't know how many sergeants this happened to—hopefully not many. You say, "Dawson, what's the point?" These soldiers would not follow their sergeant into certain death. But stay with me—Jesus never tried to "shoot the Father in the back." He followed Him to the point of death, even death on a cross.

Let's remind ourselves, one more time, of the physical realities of Christ's suffering. Frederic Farrar wrote:

> A death by crucifixion seems to include all that pain and death can have of the horrible and ghastly—dizziness, cramp, thirst, starvation, sleeplessness, traumatic fever, shame, publicity of shame, long continuance of torment, horror of anticipation, mortification of intended wounds—all intensified just up to the point which would give to the sufferer the relief of unconsciousness . . . The unnatural position made every movement painful: the lacerated veins and crushed tendons throbbed with incessant anguish.[3]

The apostle Paul said, "You must have the same attitude that Christ Jesus had" (Phil. 2:5 NLT). In other words, we are to be as committed to Jesus Christ as He was to the Father. Remember Jesus' words in Matthew 16:24: "If anyone wishes to come after Me, he must deny himself and take up his cross and follow Me" (NASB).

Let's review for a moment. Jesus was willing to obey the Father, even though it cost Him everything. In Philippians 2:5–11 we're told of Jesus' humbling steps down. These steps are illustrated by the following phrases:

- He "did not consider equality with God something to be grasped" (v. 6 NIV).
- He "emptied Himself" (v. 7 NASB).
- He "took the form of a bondservant" (v. 8 NKJV).
- He was "found in appearance as a man" (v. 8 NIV).
- He "humbled Himself" (v. 8 NKJV).
- He "became obedient to the point of death" (v. 8 NKJV).

Here are a few things that should fill our hearts in light of Jesus' sacrifice:

- *Awe* at how the Son of God was willing to submit Himself to the depths of suffering and humiliation.
- *Sadness,* even tears, at what He experienced at the hands of sinful men.
- *Remorse* for the sins we've committed that caused Him such pain.
- *Joy* that God loves us to this degree.
- *Praise* to the One who is holy, pure, and worthy of all praise.

Yes, Christ's humiliation was great. But His reward from the Father was even greater, as we'll see in the final two chapters.

17

To Even Greater Riches

In Philippians 2:5–8, the apostle Paul described the humbling steps Christ took in order to do the Father's will. In verses 9–11 he then explained the Father's actions in honoring the Son for His great accomplishments on earth: "For this reason also, God highly exalted Him, and bestowed on Him the name which is above every name" (Phil. 2:9 NASB).

We're told the Father "highly exalted" the Son, lifting Him to the heights of heaven. What does this phrase "highly exalted" mean? It's found only here in the entire New Testament. It literally means "to super-exalt"[1] or "to be lifted up beyond all measure."[2] We better understand this term when we compare various English translations and paraphrases. As stated above, the NASB says "God highly exalted Him"; the NIV says "God exalted him to the highest place"; *The Message* says "God lifted him high and honored him far beyond anyone or anything, ever." If we were to combine them all, it might read like this: *For this reason, God has exalted Christ by lifting Him to the very highest place of the heights of heaven and by honoring Him far beyond anyone or anything, ever.*

There is no comparison between the honors given on earth and the exaltation of Jesus Christ. In fact, the combination of all the honors and glory man has ever received pale in comparison to what the Father has given to Jesus Christ. Neither words nor human calculations can describe the heights to which the Father has elevated the Son.

GOD'S SPIRITUAL LAWS

Why did God the Father exalt His Son, Jesus, to the heights of heaven? First, because Jesus' life and death proved true one of God's basic spiritual laws. Just as there are laws that govern the physical universe, there are also laws that govern the spiritual realm (i.e., God's kingdom). For instance, physical laws would include the law of gravity (what goes up must come down); the law of consumption (that which is consumed is gone); and the law of necessity (human life needs food, water, and oxygen in order to live). Spiritual laws would include: the wages of sin is death (see Rom. 6:23); you reap what you sow (see Gal. 6:7–8); and the humble will be exalted (see Matt. 23:12). The Father elevated the Son because Jesus' life and death proved one of

God's unbending, never-changing laws: *The way to exaltation is always through humiliation.*

In other words, the awesome exaltation of Christ was proportionate to His humiliation. Put another way, the crown always follows the cross. Someone wrote that Christ "experienced the glory which followed the grind; the eternal sunshine which followed the earthly night."[3] Actually, this was a principle Christ had taught throughout His earthly ministry: "Whoever exalts himself will be humbled, and whoever humbles himself will be exalted" (Matt. 23:12 NIV).

It seems that even rough-hewn, boastful Peter learned this lesson along the way, for he wrote in the New Testament: "Humble yourselves under the mighty hand of God, that He may exalt you at the proper time" (1 Pet. 5:6 NASB).

In God's economy this law holds true: *The way to exaltation is always through humiliation.*

JESUS: SUPREME JUDGE

It's not possible for Jesus to become more divine or more perfect than He already is. As we know from previous chapters, there never has been nor ever will be anyone remotely like Him. Yet when the Father exalted Him Jesus was given even more privileges, honors, titles, and responsibilities than He'd had before the Cross. He regained everything He'd laid aside by coming to earth, plus much more.

For example, Jesus has now been exalted to the position of supreme Judge. The Bible teaches that every person's eternal destiny will be decided by Him, at the end of time. Every person who has ever lived will come face-to-face with Jesus Christ. This is made clear from verses such as the following:

> The Father judges no one, but has entrusted all judgment to the Son, that all may honor the Son just as they honor the Father. (John 5:22–23 NIV)

> We must all appear before the judgment seat of Christ, that each one may receive what is due him for the things done while in the body, whether good or bad. (2 Cor. 5:10 NIV)

FOREVER LINKED TO HUMANITY

Yes, Jesus lived on earth as the perfect God-man. Yet many don't realize He continues to exist today, in His resurrection state, as both God and Man. Because of His great love for us, He will live forever in a resurrected body, forever linked to those who believe in Him. What was once His humiliation, taking on the excess baggage of human nature and a judged body, has now become a reason for His exaltation. He is our eternal representative and friend.

Not only is Jesus our supreme Judge, He is also our

eternal Intercessor, as we learn in Hebrews 7:25: "He is able also to save forever those who draw near to God through Him, since He always lives to make intercession for them" (NASB). An intercessor is someone who goes before an authority on behalf of another. Jesus is our eternal Intercessor, for He will forever represent us before God.

Thankfully, Jesus is more than Judge and Intercessor; He is also our friend. He walked among us on earth that we might walk with Him in heaven. As He told His disciples in John 15:13, "Greater love has no one than this, that one lay down his life for his friends" (NASB). In every way possible, Jesus has proven His friendship to those who are saved. He bore the shame and agony of the Cross that we might be His friends forever.

Jesus is now in heaven, and God has honored Him far beyond anyone or anything, ever. Is it any wonder, then, that in heaven we will forever sing His praises and rejoice at His exaltation? Revelation 5:13 tells us of that wonderful day: "I heard every creature in heaven and on earth and under the earth and in the sea, and all that is in them, singing: 'To him who sits on the throne and to the Lamb be praise and honor and glory and power, for ever and ever!'" (NIV).

JESUS' GREAT HONOR

God the Father has always been pleased with the Son, is that not true? We see an example of this at Jesus' baptism.

We're told that after He'd been baptized by John the Baptist, "the heavens were opened to Him, and He saw the Spirit of God descending like a dove and alighting upon Him. And suddenly a voice came from heaven, saying, 'This is My beloved Son, in whom I am well pleased'" (Matt. 3:16–17 NKJV). A similar thing happened when Jesus was on the Mount of Transfiguration: "While he was still speaking, behold, a bright cloud overshadowed them; and suddenly a voice came out of the cloud, saying, 'This is My beloved Son, in whom I am well pleased. Hear Him!'" (Matt. 17:5 NKJV).

Yes, the Father was pleased with the Son at all times. Yet He was never more pleased than when Jesus breathed His last upon the cross, having won the victory over sin. I believe at that moment God gave His Son the greatest reward that could be given to anyone, anywhere, anytime. What reward was this? Paul tells us in Philippians 2:9, saying, "God highly exalted Him, and bestowed on Him the name which is above every name" (NASB). Before we look at this reward in detail, however, let's first look at God's act of giving.

What does it mean "to bestow"? The Greek word for "bestow" literally means "to give wholeheartedly,"[4] "to give graciously and freely."[5] Just as Jesus gave freely of Himself to the Father, the Father freely gave of Himself to the Son. He gave the Son the highest of all honors. Think about this: The Father was able to "bestow" this reward on the Son because the Son had "emptied Himself." If He'd not done so, He'd have been in no position to receive this awesome acknowledgment. Imagine the joy of the Father as He rewarded His Son's faithfulness!

Can you remember a time when you freely honored another person? The word *honored,* by the way, connotes "lifting up." For instance, when the Bible tells us to honor our parents, it means we are to lift them up—to treat them with high value—as though they are a gift to us, which they are. So, how have you honored others in your life?

The Bible tells us to "take delight in honoring each other" (Rom. 12:10 TLB). When I was just a kid I remember a certain woman in my father's church named Evelyn Weber. Years later, while preparing to speak at a church in California named Redwood Chapel, I found that Evelyn had moved to California and was now a member of the church's staff. I remembered Evelyn because of her passion for prayer—she was one of the greatest prayer warriors I'd ever met. As I got up to speak for the morning service I asked the crowd, "Does anyone here have a camera?" When several people raised their hands, I said, "I want you to come down here and take a picture. There's a real hero of the faith here today, and I want to tell you who it is." I invited Evelyn to come forward, and as she came I recounted the impact she'd had on that little church back in Illinois. I let them know that if I ever planted a church—or walked down a back alley at midnight—I would want this little woman next to me. The flashbulbs popped and the crowd clapped. It was an awesome moment.

Evelyn's daughter lives in Nashville, and about three weeks later she called me and said, "I want to thank you for honoring my mother." The Bible tells us to delight in honoring one another, just as the Father graciously bestowed honor on His Son with a great reward. It's a thrill to be honored. It moves us and humbles us; it also strengthens us.

Often I'll take time on our radio show, *Dawson McAllister Live,* to have what we call our "Parents Hall of Fame." I ask students to call in and say why their parents are doing a great job. At first I thought it might be a corny idea, but it works great. We do this for grandparents as well, and always get good reviews. It's important to honor special people in our lives.

THE JEALOUSY OF SAUL

God the Father was not like King Saul of the Old Testament. The people of Israel wanted a king. At first God said no, but as they continued to complain He gave in to their demands. "Okay," He said, "I'll give you what you want . . . but you won't like having a king once you get one." He gave them Saul, who was six-foot-six and awesome in every way. Unfortunately, he became prideful and wandered far from God. He eventually got so low as to consult a medium, remember that? Due to his disobedience and hardened heart, God said, "Hey, buddy—you're out of the pool. I'm going to give your throne to somebody else."

The person God chose to replace Saul was named David, a shepherd boy who tended sheep in the hills of Bethlehem. This is the little guy who struck down Goliath with just a rock and a slingshot. This didn't make Saul happy, especially when the people began to dance and sing, "Saul has slain his thousands, and David his tens of thousands" (1 Sam. 18:7 NIV). In fact, Saul became very angry (you might say "royally ticked-off"), and from that time on he kept a jealous eye on David. Time won't allow us to explore all the contrasts here, but God the Father was never jealous of Jesus' success. Rather, He was totally at peace, rejoicing in His Son's accomplishments. He did not ask the cynical question, as did Saul, "How much more can He get of the kingdom!" Instead He asked, "How much more of the kingdom can I give to My Son?" The Father was not annoyed . . . He was thrilled!

It's natural for sons to honor fathers and fathers to honor their sons. Men, don't you each long for your father's approval? Several years ago I had the privilege of speaking at Thomas Road Baptist Church, the church founded by Jerry Falwell. My dad, a godly man who is my hero, loved Jerry Falwell. So, while sitting on the platform I spied a photographer in the audience. As I got up to speak I said, "Jerry, will you do me a favor? Would you come up here behind the pulpit with me?" He graciously did so, not sure what I had in mind. "Jerry," I continued, "I'd like that photographer to take a picture of us right here before I speak. My dad thinks you're a hero. I'd love to have a picture of us here today so I can give it to my dad. I want him to be proud of me." The whole place went crazy. Everybody wants to be honored by their father. What a joy it was to give that picture to my dad.

JESUS' NAME ABOVE ALL

Getting back to the Philippians passage, Paul continued by saying, ". . . and bestowed on Him the name which is above every name" (2:9 NASB). What great honor did the Father bestow on the Son? He gave Him a name above every name ever spoken.

You may say, "Dawson, is that it? That's the reward Jesus received for all His suffering on earth?" Yes, that's it. But let's understand the extreme importance of what this means. In ancient times a person's name often implied profound meaning. For instance, the Greek word *onoma,* or "name," "was not only a means of distinguishing one individual from another, but also a means of revealing the inner being, the true nature of that individual."[6] Parents didn't look in a book and say, "Hey, what kind of trendy name can we give our kid?" No, they gave their child a name that had meaning behind it: a character trait to live up to, or perhaps a name that described the circumstances of the time. As someone once said, names in that day were more than titles; they described the total essence of a person's inner being. Names meant something.

Some of you will remember Cassius Clay, a boxer who in the mid-1960s changed his name to Muhammad Ali. He made this change because he converted to Islam, but also because he had something to prove. He said, "Cassius Clay is a slave's name; I didn't choose it and I didn't want it. I am Muhammad Ali, which is a free name meaning 'beloved of God.' I insist people use it when speaking to me and of me."[7] Around that time Ali fought a guy named Ernie Terrell. During the prefight buildup, Terrell refused to call his opponent by his new name—he insisted on calling him Cassius Clay. Well, you may remember what happened. Over the course of twelve rounds, Ali beat Terrell to a pulp. As he hit Terrell time and again with his lightning-fast jab, beating his face to mush, Ali would yell out, "What's my name, fool, what's my name?" Ali took his name very seriously, and no one called him Cassius Clay again.

In the ancient Near East names had such significance they were often changed in order to better fit the person. Abram, which means "father," was changed to Abraham—"father of many." Jacob ("deceiver") was renamed Israel ("rules with God") after wrestling with God. And Jesus changed the name of Simon ("volatile") to Peter ("rock") at a significant point in his life. Names were changed to better reflect a person's character.

JESUS CHRIST THE LORD

When it comes to Jesus, the Bible refers to Him by more than 250 different names.[8] Each one of them is important, describing in some way the awesomeness of His being. Like the many sides of a sparkling diamond, each of these names describes a particular aspect of His multifaceted glory. Here are just a few examples of those found in Scripture:

- Almighty (Rev. 1:8 NIV)
- Alpha and Omega (see Rev. 1:8)
- Arm of the LORD (Isa. 51:9 NIV)
- Bread of Life (John 6:48 NIV)
- Bright and Morning Star (Rev. 22:16 NKJV)
- Chief Cornerstone (1 Pet. 2:6 NKJV)
- Brightness of Father's Glory (see Heb. 1:3)
- Truth (John 14:6 NIV)
- Immanuel (Isa. 7:14 NIV)
- Eternal Life (1 John 5:20 NIV)

All these great names given to the Son, and many more, stir love and reverence in our hearts. When you're that great—when you need 250 names to just begin to describe you—you're no small thing. We're not talking about some Boy Scout with a little halo on his head, who came to help little old ladies across the Sea of Galilee!

We're talking about the Almighty. Yet the Bible says there is a name that rises far above all others. What is the name above every name? We find it as we come to the last verse of our passage in Philippians 2: "That every tongue will confess that Jesus Christ is Lord, to the glory of God the Father" (v. 11 NASB).

The name above every name is: **JESUS CHRIST THE LORD.** This name is so deep, so profound, we must examine each part separately.

THE NAME *JESUS*

The name *Jesus* is a religious name. It comes from the Hebrew word for "Joshua," and some say it was as common in Jesus' day as the name Josh is today. What did it mean? "Jehovah saves." You can be sure, however, those Jewish parents who named their sons Jesus didn't understand what that name would later mean to the world. When the angel appeared to Joseph in a dream, he said, "You are to give him the name Jesus, because he will save his people from their sins" (Matt. 1:21 NIV). This common name would hold uncommon significance because of this little baby. This was made known even before His birth.

Why do you think the name *Jesus* is so powerful? Though many boys over the centuries have been named Jesus or Joshua, only one of them came to save His people from their sins. Only *this* Jesus can give us peace with God. I'm reminded of when Peter spoke to the crowd after Jesus' resurrection: "Let all Israel be assured of this: God has made this Jesus, whom you crucified, both Lord and Christ" (Acts 2:36 NIV). Not any Jesus, but "this" Jesus. God took the name *Jesus* and pumped real life into it.

THE NAME *CHRIST*

The name *Christ* is a Greek translation of the Hebrew word *Messiah.* It literally means "anointed one"[9]—the One who will set his people free. In the Old Testament the prophets foretold His coming, prophesying that the Messiah would deliver His people from bondage. One source states, "For centuries the Jewish people had looked for the prophesied Messiah, a deliverer who would usher in a kingdom of peace and prosperity."[10] The prophet Isaiah said this about the One who was coming:

> To us a child is born,
>   to us a son is given,
>   and the government will be on his shoulders.
> And he will be called Wonderful Counselor,
>   Mighty God,
>   Everlasting Father, Prince of Peace.
> Of the increase of his government and peace
>   there will be no end.

He will reign on David's throne
  and over his kingdom,
establishing and upholding it
  with justice and righteousness
  from that time on and forever.
The zeal of the LORD Almighty
  will accomplish this. (Isa. 9:6–7 NIV)

Tragically, most Jews today are still looking for the appearance of the Messiah. They reject the truth of Jesus Christ, refusing to believe He was God's chosen Messiah. Most consider Jesus to be a fraud. However, Christ made it abundantly clear He was God's Anointed One:

> When Jesus came to the region of Caesarea Philippi, he asked his disciples, "Who do people say the Son of Man is?"
>
> They replied, "Some say John the Baptist; others say Elijah; and still others, Jeremiah or one of the prophets."
>
> "But what about you?" he asked. "Who do you say I am?"
>
> Simon Peter answered, "You are the Christ, the Son of the living God."
>
> Jesus replied, "Blessed are you, Simon son of Jonah, for this was not revealed to you by man, but by my Father in heaven." (Matt. 16:13–17 NIV)

Again, as Jesus stood before the leaders of Israel on the night before His crucifixion, He resolutely claimed this title. The high priest looked Him right in the eyes and said, "Are You the Christ? The Son of the Blessed?" Jesus' life hung in the balance. He responded by saying, "I am, and the next time you see Me you'll see Me coming on the clouds of heaven." That's all these leaders needed to hear. They accused Him of blasphemy, tore their robes, and sentenced Him to death. Christ's own people rejected Him, but now in heaven our Savior carries this "name which is above every name." He is the Christ, forever praised as the Anointed One, the Messiah.

HIS NAME IS *LORD*

Finally, let's look at the name *Lord.* The Greek word is *kurios,* and it literally means "master; one who rules or exercises authority over others."[11] In referring to Christ, it means "God, the one who commands us."[12] Jesus is Lord of all—He's in absolute control of the entire universe. He has all authority over heaven and earth (see Matt. 28:18). When Jesus was awarded the title of Lord, He was given the ultimate name. It's the greatest title Jesus could have received, for it covers everything. The great I AM stands above all other leaders, all other kings, all other sovereigns. He's not just *a* lord—He is King of all kings, and Lord of all lords.

We're told in Revelation 19:15–16 that when Jesus Christ comes again to this earth, "'He will rule them with an iron scepter.' He treads the winepress of the fury of the wrath of God Almighty. On his robe and on his thigh he has this name written: KING OF KINGS AND LORD OF LORDS" (NIV).

As a faithful Son, Jesus received the greatest reward ever given. This Jesus, who is the Christ—the Anointed One—has been given all authority in the universe to rule as Lord. What can you and I do, but submit to such an awesome and loving God?

18

Christ's Final Exaltation

We've now arrived at the end of this amazing passage: "So that at the name of Jesus every knee will bow, of those who are in heaven and on earth and under the earth, and that every tongue will confess that Jesus Christ is Lord, to the glory of God the Father" (Phil. 2:10–11 NASB).

These last verses inform us that the ultimate conclusion to Jesus' obedience and humiliation will eternally affect every person, everywhere. Every created being will encounter the name of Jesus, and will bow and confess Him as Lord of all. As we learned in the previous chapter, "Jesus Christ the Lord" is the ultimate name in the universe. It's not just a title; it describes the total of all that Jesus is—His preeminence and authority over all things. What does it mean that "every knee will bow" at His name? It's not the name itself that will bring all creatures to their knees, but rather the authority His name signifies.

Every created being will bow before Him, thus paying the deepest respect.

Several years ago I was in a magazine shop at O'Hare airport, killing time between flights. As I approached the counter to buy something I heard a man behind me cussing a blue streak. He was saying "Jesus Christ this" and "Jesus Christ that." It was over the top, and finally I'd had my fill. I went over to him and said, "Man, I keep hearing you mention the name Jesus Christ. He must have really done something great for you—can you tell me what it is?" That dude looked at me for a second then took off running down the airport concourse. Who knows where he is today, but I know that someday he will encounter the name of Jesus and realize it's more than a swearword.

PAYING ULTIMATE RESPECT

At Christ's second coming all people will pay their respects to Jesus Christ—both friend and foe. The Bible tells us there will be a massive gathering of all creatures, "those who are in heaven and on earth and under the earth" (Phil. 2:10 NASB). But what does this mean? Who are these created beings Paul mentions in this passage? I like to refer to this classification as "upstairs, downstairs, and in the basement." Let me explain.

"Those who are in heaven" (upstairs) would include all believers who have died and gone to be with Christ.

Theologians call these people "departed saints." They were born again in this life then died and went to heaven, be they great or small, king or pauper, men or women, old or young. It also includes heavenly angels, created beings often referred to as "ministering servants," or "messengers." God made them to serve and worship Him, and heaven echoes their songs of praise at all times (see Isa. 6:1–3). How many angels are there? We don't know for sure, but in Revelation 5:11–12 we gain a glimpse into the vast number of angelic hosts:

> I looked and heard the voice of many angels, numbering thousands upon thousands, and ten thousand times ten thousand. They encircled the throne and the living creatures and the elders. In a loud voice they sang,
>
> "Worthy is the Lamb, who was slain,
> to receive power and wealth and wisdom and
> strength
> and honor and glory and praise!" (NIV)

If my math is correct, that's more than one hundred million angels all gathered around the throne of God. That's a lot of wings—and more important, a lot of praise to our Lord Jesus Christ.

So upstairs we have angels and humans who are now with Christ. What about downstairs, or those "on the earth"? These are people, both Christians and non-Christians, who will be alive on the earth at Christ's second coming. The Bible refers to them in 2 Thessalonians:

> This will happen when the Lord Jesus is revealed from heaven in blazing fire with his powerful angels. He will punish those who do not know God and do not obey the gospel of our Lord Jesus. They will be punished with everlasting destruction and shut out from the presence of the Lord and from the majesty of his power on the day he comes to be glorified in his holy people and to be marveled at among all those who have believed. (1:7b–10a NIV)

Some of these, the believers in Jesus, will be rewarded with eternal life. Those who are unbelievers, who "do not obey the gospel," will be cast into hell, shut out from God's presence for all eternity. That truly is the definition of hell, isn't it? Hell is a place where God and His benefits are unknown; a place where sin will be punished for forever and ever.

What about those in the basement, or "under the earth"? These are beings currently held in the underworld, including all fallen angels (demons) as well as humans who have previously died apart from Christ. This includes Satan himself, one of the most powerful angels of all, who rebelled against God and took a third of the angels with him. In Revelation 20:12–13 we're told of an event called "the Great White Throne Judgment." This will take place at the end of time, and it's where many theologians believe every knee and tongue will be forced to acknowledge Christ's lordship. Here's what it says: "I saw the dead, great and small, standing before the throne . . . The sea gave up the dead that were in it, and death and Hades gave up the dead that were in them, and each person was judged according to what he had done" (NIV).

Some may say, "Dawson, what's Hades? What and where is that?" Hades is God's county jail. It's a holding area for all who have died apart from Christ, until they stand before the Great White Throne where final judgment will take place.

Who else is "under the earth"? The demons who are now imprisoned. The Bible tells us some demons are so vile, so repugnant, they have been bound in prison until the time of final judgment. We're told in 1 Peter 3:19 that Jesus, after His death, "went and preached to the spirits in prison" (NIV). We're told some of these demons will be released during the coming Tribulation period to wreak havoc on the earth. Yet ultimately they too will bow before Jesus Christ and will be punished for all eternity. Who, then, will pay homage to Jesus Christ as Lord? Every being ever created—upstairs, downstairs, and in the basement.

EVERY KNEE WILL BOW

What does it mean that every knee will bow before Jesus Christ? As you may know, kneeling is an ancient tradition. In the Bible we first see it in the time of Abraham, when we're told he knelt before God (see Gen. 18:2). It says when God appeared Abraham bowed low to the ground. Kneeling is an act of great humility and deep religious devotion. One source says of kneeling, "It involved prostration, the practice of falling upon the knees, gradually inclining the body, and touching the forehead to the ground."[1] I read somewhere that more than 105 billion people have lived on this earth. When we include all angels, that's a lot of created beings kneeling before Jesus, isn't it? What an amazing sight that will be!

The closest picture we have of this in the Bible is at the dedication of Solomon's temple in the Old Testament. We're told that a massive "bowing down" took place:

> When Solomon finished praying, fire came down from heaven and consumed the burnt offering and the sacrifices, and the glory of the LORD filled the temple. The priests could not enter the temple of the LORD because the glory of the LORD filled it. When all the Israelites saw the fire coming down and the glory of the LORD above the temple, they knelt on the pavement with their faces to

> the ground, and they worshiped and gave thanks to the LORD, saying, "He is good; his love endures forever." (2 Chron. 7:1–3 NIV)

It's obvious Jesus Christ deserves, and will one day receive, all glory and honor and tremendous worship. One day everyone, not just our Pentecostal friends, will show an outward expression of respect for Jesus Christ. Yet this act by itself will not be enough; God will demand that every person, every creature, verbally confess Jesus Christ as Lord.

THE HIGHEST CONFESSION

For all you married men, and those of you who are dating, can you imagine trying to win a woman's heart with only a gesture? Imagine that you knock on her door, she answers, and then you smile and wave—and that's it. Does that win points? Of course not. You need the spoken language of love in order to win her heart. Ultimately, God will command that each creature confess Jesus as Lord, either by choice or by force. There are approximately sixty-nine hundred different languages and dialects in our modern world.[2] This means the great confession of Christ's lordship will be spoken nearly seven thousand different ways. What a beautiful noise that will be!

"Confess" means "to intensely agree with," or "to admit a truth publicly."[3] Though the greatness and glory of Jesus are currently muffled on earth, one day all creation will roar in agreement that He is Lord of all things. There will be nothing muffled about it! One time my wife, Ruth Hill, and I were at a gathering in Seoul, South Korea. At the time it was called the largest gathering in history—nearly 2.7 million people attended. How big is that? It took place in a marching field that was half a mile wide by a mile and a half long. My buddy and I were at one end of the crowd, and there's no way we could see the other side. On that day I learned there are two exclamations that are universal: "Hallelujah!" and "Praise the Lord!" Loudspeakers were scattered throughout the grounds, and when a Korean preacher stood up to speak he yelled, "Hallelujah!" With one voice the massive crowd shouted back, "Hallelujah!" It was like thunder!

Can you imagine what it's going to be like in heaven? This great confession will be the most beautiful thing we've ever heard. So I ask you, what does it mean that every knee will bow and every tongue will confess that Jesus is Lord? Let me quote John MacArthur, who summarizes this passage well:

> Christ will no longer be acknowledged as servant but as Lord of all. One day all creatures will wholeheartedly agree that Jesus Christ is all he claimed to be—God. Every created being will admit the truth either voluntarily or by compulsion. Every personal being will ultimately confess

> Christ's lordship, either with joyful faith or with resentment and despair.[4]

Even hostile demons and Satan himself will have no choice but to confess and agree that Jesus Christ is Lord.

THE MOST IMPORTANT DECISION

Friend, everyone's going to confess Christ's lordship one way or the other. If you haven't yet accepted Christ as Lord of your life, I pray you will do so soon. Romans 10:9–10 tells us: "If you confess with your mouth, 'Jesus is Lord,' and believe in your heart that God raised him from the dead, you will be saved. For it is with your heart that you believe and are justified, and it is with your mouth that you confess and are saved" (NIV).

Right now—today—you have the opportunity to receive Him as Lord and Savior. After you die, or when Christ comes back, it will be too late. One time I shared Christ with a man who became hostile toward me. He said, "I'll deal with God when I see Him." I told him that wasn't a good idea—that'd he'd lose. He looked at me and responded, "I think you're wrong, but I guess we'll find out when the bugle blows, won't we?" At that point it's too late—it's too late. On the Day of Judgment, billions upon billions of people will correctly confess that Jesus is Lord, but for those who are unsaved it will do them no good. Their hope of peace with God will be gone forever.

Some may say, "Dawson, I've prayed a prayer to God. Is that all I have to do to be saved?" Yes and no. God responds to the prayer that is sincere. Prayer must be more than speaking correct words to God; it must involve a decision of the heart, followed by life-change. As we saw, Jesus said, "On that day many will say to me, 'Lord, Lord, did we not prophesy in your name, and cast out demons in your name, and do many mighty works in your name?' And then I will declare to them, 'I never knew you; depart from me, you workers of lawlessness'" (Matt. 7:22–23 ESV).

Some believe that up to 70 percent of individuals who attend evangelical churches do not know Christ personally. Salvation is not found in "being religious" or in doing good things. It's found in a personal relationship with Jesus Christ.

So let me ask you—do you know Him? Take an honest look at your own heart, then ask yourself this question: "Have I placed my complete trust in Jesus Christ and the work He accomplished on the cross on my behalf? Not faith in the church—but in Jesus. Not in my religious deeds—but in Jesus. Not in my parents' expression of faith—but in Jesus." The answer to this question will determine your eternal destiny. If the answer is no—or you're not sure what this question means—may I encourage you to ask the Lord into your heart right now. Here is a simple prayer that might guide your words as you sincerely pour out your heart to God:

God, I realize that I am a sinner, and that my sins have separated me from an eternity in Your presence. I understand that Jesus died in my place on the cross, and that He paid the debt for all my sins. I now accept You into my heart and my life. I turn from those things that displease You, and I ask You to lead me; please help me to follow. Come and change me forever, and have Your way in my life. Thank You for hearing this prayer. I pray this in Jesus' name, amen.

Friend, if you sincerely prayed this simple prayer to God, and meant it with all your heart, I can now call you my brother or sister in Christ! Congratulations on finding a new life in Jesus Christ. Please, share your decision with a Christian friend or pastor, and get involved in a church near you that teaches the Bible. This will help you grow in your newfound faith. You have a wonderful journey ahead of you!

For those who already know Christ personally, let me encourage you to do something important. Take a sheet of paper and make a list of people you know who aren't yet born again. Pray for them by name, and ask God for opportunities to share how they can have peace with God. The Bible says, "It's a terrifying thing to fall into the hands of the living God" (Heb. 10:31 NASB). Be faithful in praying for your unsaved friends and family—you never know how God will use you.

Conclusion

It has been my privilege, by way of this book, to have you join me in this walk with Christ to the Cross. We've seen His amazing love and His tender compassion. We've marveled at His single-minded determination to do the Father's will, no matter what the cost. Perhaps we've wept as we've gazed at the beautiful Son of God, broken and bleeding on a Roman tool of torture—the cross. Jesus completed His mission by taking unbelievable steps downward, laying aside His divine perks and privileges—suffering the worst of humiliations. Yet God did not abandon Him forever. At the right time He exalted Jesus to a place of incredible honor and authority, where He remains today as our supreme Judge, Intercessor, and Friend.

Let's live our lives in such a way as to honor His great sacrifice. And let's remember the great truth He taught by word and example:

The way to exaltation is always through humiliation.

Notes

Chapter 2: Peter Will Be "Sifted"

1 James Strong, *The New Strong's Complete Dictionary of Bible Words* (Nashville: Thomas Nelson, 1996), 698.
2 *The Preacher's Outline and Sermon Bible:* vol. 4, *Luke* (Chattanooga, TN: Leadership Ministries Worldwide, 1991).
3 John Piper, "The Sifting of Simon Peter" (Bethlehem Baptist Church, 1981), http://www.soundofgrace.com/piper81/042681m.htm.

Chapter 3: Jesus in Agony at Gethsemane

1 Guttmacher Institute, "U.S. Teenage Pregnancy Statistics National and State Trends and Trends by Race and Ethnicity," http://www.guttmacher.org/pubs/2006/09/12/USTPstats.pdf (accessed March 25, 2008).

Chapter 4: The Pride and Prayerlessness of Peter

1 William Hendriksen, *The New Testament Commentary: Matthew* (Grand Rapids, MI: Baker Books, 1973), 914.
2 Charles H. Spurgeon, *The King Has Come: A Commentary on Matthew* (Old Tappan, NJ: 1987).
3 *The Preacher's Outline and Sermon Bible.*

4 John F. MacArthur, *The MacArthur New Testament Commentary: Matthew*. CD-ROM. Quickverse, 2005.
5 Strong, *New Strong's Complete Dictionary*, 598.
6 MacArthur, *MacArthur New Testament Commentary: Matthew.*
7 *The Preacher's Outline and Sermon Bible: Matthew.*

Chapter 5: An Awestruck Crowd

1 Alfred Edersheim, *The Life and Times of Jesus the Messiah*, vol. 1 (Grand Rapids, MI: Eerdmans, 1980), 263.

Chapter 6: Peter Tries to Follow Jesus Incognito

1 R. C. H. Lenski, *Commentary on the New Testament: John* (Peabody, MA: Hendrickson, 2001), 1194.
2 Ibid., 1087.
3 Frank Gaebelein, ed., *The Expositor's Bible Commentary: Luke.* CD-ROM. Zondervan Software, 1997.
4 Spurgeon, *Commentary on Matthew.*
5 William Barclay, *The Daily Bible Study Series: Luke* (Edinburgh: St. Andrews Press, 1953).
6 MacArthur, *The MacArthur New Testament Commentary.*
7 H. D. M. Spence and Joseph S. Excell, eds., *Pulpit Commentary*, vol. 15, *Matthew* (Grand Rapids, MI: Eerdmans 1983).
8 Strong, *New Strong's Complete Dictionary*, 614.

Chapter 7: Jesus Confronts Hard Hearts

1 William Whiston, trans., *The Complete Works of Josephus* (Grand Rapids, MI: Kregel, 1978), 388.
2 Ibid., 379, 479.

Chapter 8: Pilate Panics

1 Alfred Edersheim, *The Life and Times of Jesus the Messiah*, part 2 (Grand Rapids, MI: Eerdmans, 1980), 587.
2 Strong, *New Strong's Complete Dictionary*, 591.

Chapter 9: Last-Minute Repentance

1 Strong, *New Strong's Complete Dictionary,* 495.

Chapter 10: A Cry Out of the Darkness

1 Strong, *New Strong's Complete Dictionary,* 711.

Chapter 11: The Restoration of Peter

1 William Barclay, *The Daily Bible Study Series: Mark* 2nd ed. (Philadelphia: Westminster, 1956), 389.
2 For a discussion on the two words for "love" found in John 21:15–17, see the following resource: W. E. Vine, *The Expanded Vine's Expository Dictionary of New Testament Words* (Minneapolis: Bethany House, 1984), 694.
3 Strong, *New Strong's Complete Dictionary,* 721.
4 *The Preacher's Outline and Sermon Bible: John.*
5 Ibid.

Chapter 12: A Great Encounter

1 Merrill Frederick Unger, *The New Unger's Bible Dictionary* (Chicago, IL: Moody Press), 1988.
2 "Resurrection Event Timeline" is adapted from John Phillips, *Exploring the Gospel of John* (Grand Rapids, MI: Kregel, 1989), 376–77.
3 George R. Beasley-Murray, *Word Biblical Commentary: John,* vol. 36 (Dallas, TX: Word, 1987), 374.
4 Adam Clarke, *A Commentary on the Holy Bible—One Volume Edition* (Grand Rapids, MI: Baker, 1967).

Chapter 13: He Made Himself Nothing

1 J. D. Douglas, ed., *New Commentary on the Whole Bible,* rev. ed. (Wheaton, IL: 1990).
2 Strong, *New Strong's Complete Dictionary,* 645.

3 Ibid.

4 Timothy and Barbara Friberg, Analytical Lexicon to the Greek New Testament (ANLEX). CD-ROM. Hermeneutika Computer Bible Research Softerware, 1994, 1996.

5 W. Arndt, F. W. Gingrich, F. W. Danker, and W. Bauer, *A Greek-English Lexicon of the New Testament and Other Early Christian Literature: A Translation and Adaptation of the Fourth Revised and Augmented Edition of Walter Bauer's Griechisch-deutsches Worterbuch zu den Schrift en des Neuen Testaments und der ubrigen urchristlichen Literatur,* 2nd ed., rev. and augmented. CD-ROM. University of Chicago Press, 1979. Logos Research Systems Bible Library, 2000–2006.

Chapter 14: He Laid Aside His Glory and Riches

1 James Strong, *Enhanced Strong's Lexicon* (Oak Harbor, WA: Logos Research Systems), 1995.

2 "Childproof Prevention" Web site, http://www.safekidsbc.ca/statistics.htm. Under the section titled "The Impact of Abuse," it says: "In 1999, the McCreary Adolescent Health Survey II found that 35% of girls and 16% of boys between grades 7-12 have been sexually and/or physically abused."

Chapter 15: He Took on Humanity

1 John F. MacArthur, *The MacArthur New Testament Commentary: Philippians* (Chicago, IL: Moody Press, 2001), 130.

2 Strong, *New Strong's Complete Dictionary,* 627.

3 Ibid., 709.

Chapter 16: He Died a Horrible Death

1 Strong, *New Strong's Complete Dictionary,* 710.

2 Dwight Edwards, "Philippians: Earthly Conduct of Heavenly Citizens" http://bible.org/page.php?page_id=1428. Accessed on March 25, 2008.

3 Frederic Farrar, *The Life of Christ,* vol. 2 (New York: E. P. Dutton, 1877), 403–4.

Chapter 17: To Even Greater Riches

1 Lawrence O. Richards, *The Victor Bible Background Commentary New Testament* (Wheaton, IL: Victor Books, 1994).
2 Strong, *Enhanced Strong's Lexicon.*
3 Edwards, "Earthly Conduct of Heavenly Citizens."
4 William Hendrikson, *The New Testament Commentary: Philippians* (Grand Rapids, MI: Baker, 1962), 115.
5 Strong, *Enhanced Strong's Lexicon.*
6 Gerald F. Hawthorne, *Word Biblical Commentary: Philippians,* vol. 43 (Dallas, TX: Word, 1998).
7 "Thousands of true funny stories about famous people," http://www.anecdotage.com/index.php?aid=7741.
8 Orville J. Nave, *Nave's Topical Bible* (Nashville, TN: Southwestern Co., 1962), 703.
9 Strong, *New Strong's Complete Dictionary.*
10 Herbert Lockyer, ed., *Nelson's Illustrated Bible Dictionary* (Nashville, TN: Thomas Nelson, 1986).
11 Johannes P. Louw and Eugene A Nida, *Greek-English Lexicon of the New Testament Based on Semantic Domains* (New York: United Bible Societies, 1988, 1989).
12 Ibid.

Chapter 18: Christ's Final Exaltation

1 Lockyer, ed., *Nelson's Illustrated BibleDictionary.*
2 http://www.ethnologue.com/ethno_docs/distribution.asp?by=area. At the bottom of the page entitled "Statistical Summaries" is a chart that lists the number of languages by continent, with 6,912 given as the total.
3 Strong, *New Strong's Complete Dictionary,* 618.
4 MacArthur, *MacArthur New Testament Commentary: Philippians,* 146.

About the Author

For more than forty years Dawson McAllister has been speaking to and for the American teenager. Born and raised in Peoria, Illinois, he graduated from Bethel College in Minnesota and then studied at Talbot Theological Seminary. When he is not hosting his radio program, *Dawson McAllister Live,* or speaking at a conference, McAllister is at home with his wife and two adopted sons. They live on a farm—McAllister's an avid horseman—just south of Nashville, Tennessee.